BROKEN LOVE

My Journey Through

Loss and Grief

MEGHANN SCULLY

Published by Book Hub Publishing

For further information re national & international distribution:
www.bookhubpublishing.com
info@bookhubpublishing.com
@BookHubPublish

Printed in the Republic of Ireland
First Edition 2018
ISBN 978-1-9998951-5-0
Cover design, book concept layout & editing by Niall McElwee
Internal design by Caroline Kenny Redmond
Cover Photograph of PEACOCK butterfly by Colin Stanley @CStanleyNature
Proofread by Karen Gallen
6th Reprint

A catalogue record for this book is available from the British Library.
This publication is sold with the understanding that the Publisher/Author is not engaged in rendering health, legal services or other professional services. If legal advice, health or other expert assistance is required, the services of a competent, qualified professional person should be sought.

ACKNOWLEDGEMENTS

I would like to take this opportunity to thank my Mammy, Pauline, for everything she has done for me and continues to do for me. She is the more than just a mother to me. She is a friend, a confidante, an advisor and she has my best interests at heart. We have gone on this journey together and I've learned so much from her. Without her I never would have had the strength or courage to face the road of grief and to write this book.

To Book Hub Publishing and, in particular, Dr Niall McElwee, my senior editor, Susan McKenna and all the team for their continued support throughout this journey. There has been a wonderful sense of community among the wider Book Hub Publishing family and it has made this experience very rewarding.

A special mention to those who gave me words of encouragement and were part of my healing.

To all my family, especially the Berminghams, who have been with me from the very start of my life. From babysitting me to helping mam rear me and for being great support and sound neighbours. Special thanks to my stepdad, Andrew, for looking after Mam and I over the years.

To all my friends who have provided me with some of the greatest memories and for being by my side through the good and the bad, thank you. To every person I have met throughout my life that have impacted me in any way.

Finally, to you the reader, I hope my story can provide you with comfort and understanding while on your journey.

DEDICATION

This book is dedicated to you.

CONTENTS

EDITOR'S INTRODUCTION

Dr. Niall McElwee, Senior Communications Consultant,
The Book Hub Publishing Group

"Death alone from death can save.
Love is death, and so is brave--
Love can fill the deepest grave.
Love loves on beneath the wave"
-George MacDonald

I have known Meghann for several years now. We are both regular attendees of our beloved Connacht rugby team at the Sportsground in Galway and have travelled on a rugby tour together to Toulouse in 2016 (sadly, Connacht were beaten in that game). She is also the daughter of one of our other Book Hub Publishing Authors, Pauline Bermingham Scully, who wrote South Galway Stories Vols 1, 2 and 3. So, a Mammy/Daughter combo no less. And, both are lovely women to be around and to work with.

Meghann writes wellness blogs for me over at bookhubpublishing.com and she consults with us over at dissertationdoctorsclinic.com. She is also scheduled to contribute a chapter in each of our five volumes in the #MentalHealthForMillennials Series in addition to co-presenting a range of workshops with us for the Clinic. Meghann has, as they say, 'form' with us.

Meghann has a national profile with her work as a broadcaster on Spin South West radio and is regularly in the public eye. I'm sure many people have an opinion of her based on what they think she is like both professionally and personally when they listen to her on her morning radio show, or watch her hosting various events. They would be wrong. There is a vulnerability and tenderness to Meghann that runs deep in her as is evident in her book and, it seems to me, Meghann veils this when presenting her public persona. She has learned to do this as grief suffocated her teenage years and stuck to her like warm oil. She wanted it to 'go away.' But, it didn't.

Indeed, one of my main challenges as her editor was to coax Meghann, in our review meetings, to tease out her profound emotionality around loss and grief and, to paraphrase Hemingway, get her to 'bleed onto the typewriter'. By doing this, her writing became more real, more evocative, more challenging and more....beautiful.

Loss and grief are immensely difficult themes to explore but Meghann does this with aplomb. She writes from her heart and one cannot but be moved by many of her observations. Her brother, Marcus, and her father, Maxie, loom large in this book, as does her utter bewilderment at their deaths and the loss of such primary and dominant male figures in her life when she was only a teenager. She has carried that loss and grief through her teens and into her twenties, at times finding it all too much whilst, at other times, being able to at least function on a day to day basis.

But, their absence cast such dark shadows over her very being that it's obvious it is only in latter years that Meghann is coming to terms with their absence in her life. Her book illustrates the importance of living life, of reaching out to family, friends, colleagues and professionals and, most of all, of being unafraid to get in touch with self.

We live in a postmodern world where most people have the opportunity and facility to filter their lives for public consumption - as noted in one of Meghann's chapters. But, each of us must live life with the inevitable occurrences that will happen around and to us. Death is but one of these. Let's have a more open conversation about death, dying and bereavement and how we might be better prepared. Bravo Meghann for this important contribution.

FOREWORD

Colette Sexton
News Correspondent at The Sunday Business Post

Meghann and I first met nearly a decade ago thanks to a bit of serendipity. Although we had both been students in University of Limerick we did not meet in the college hangouts of the Stables, the Lodge or the library. Instead, we ended up on Erasmus in Malta together in 2009. Life "studying" abroad was pretty great. Ever the dedicated students, we arranged our timetables to ensure we only had three days of college each week, and the rest of the time there was sun, sea and sand to keep us entertained. Meghann was, and is, full of life, fun and mischief.

A situation like Erasmus, where people are removed from their wider family and friend groups, can be intense but often leads to long term friendships. Luckily for me, after the pool parties and sunshine of Erasmus, I returned to UL with a firm friend in Meghann and we continued to spend a lot of time together. In our final year in UL, we both applied for the masters in journalism in NUI Galway and I still remember the call from Meghann when we realised we had both been accepted. In September 2011, four of us moved into a little house next door to NUIG which was lovely but extremely damp. Several pairs of Meghann's shoes fell victim to the mould, but don't worry, ever the keen shopper she had many, many more pairs to keep her feet covered.

We had high hopes for our time in Galway but unfortunately what was supposed to be a fantastic year ended up being the most difficult of our friendship. Despite us doing the same college course and living together, I felt pushed away from Meghann's life. She was going out a lot with new friends, and complained when the housemates wanted to stay in. At the time, I put this distance down to her being newly single and becoming friends with a new group of people. It took me a long time to realise that she was actually trying to escape from her grief.

Meghann had always been really open about speaking about her brother, Marcus who had died in a car crash and about her father, Maxie, who died the year after. When she first told me about the tragedies early on in our friendship, it seemed so shocking to me that she had been through so much at such a young age but she always seemed so strong. What Meghann learned in Galway, and what she explained to me afterwards, was that she always felt she had to be strong and therefore never really mourned over the loss of her brother and father.

In 2011, the true extent of the loss she had been through started to dawn on her. Taken away from the stability of UL and her many, many friends there, the change in environment seemed to be a trigger for Meghann to think about everything she had been through in her life. She became a different person and pushed her long term friends away.

While all of the housemates were all worried about her, I don't think any of us understood the extent of what she was going through at the time. We didn't know what to do. We supported her in going to counselling and suggested she move home to her mother for a while, but she took that to mean we did not want her around anymore. Despite how close Meghann and I were physically in college and at home, we drifted apart. After our college course ended, our communication ended too.

What once was a close friendship disappeared. We met at graduation and we were like acquaintances instead of close friends. Despite our shared history and happy memories, we knew nothing of the other person's current life. The final straw for me came in March 2013. I had moved home from a period living in England and discovered Meghann had deleted me off social media. I still had her email address and decided it was time to mend our friendship. In the email, I told her I was sorry for hurting her, for being clueless and not knowing how to help. I told her I missed her and I wanted our friendship back. In true Meghann fashion, her response back began with a joke. My email had gone into spam - thanks to my surname. We met up shortly afterwards and after some initial awkwardness, it was back to old times. Meghann told me she had an interview with MTV. When she got the job and moved to London I was delighted, but I was even more delighted when she got the job in Spin SW where she is thriving.

I am so proud of Meghann. What she went through with the loss of Marcus and Maxie was appalling but Meghann pulled herself through. She is one of the strongest people I have ever met and I always knew that she would be a success. Here I am writing the foreword for her book, and I imagine it will be the first book of many. Meghann is proof that depression and grief does not define your entire life. It is part of a story but it is not the whole book.

Broken Love is raw, emotive and heart breaking but it is also educational and inspiring. I read it in one sitting - it was impossible to put down. For you, the reader, I recommend you set aside some time to curl up with this book and some tissues. You are about to learn a lot.

Hey there,

Welcome to my first book. I'm a Galway Girl and a Limerick Lady. I was raised in Galway but studied, and now live, in Limerick. I'm telling my story about a young girl who loved and lost. That young girl is me. So, this is a deeply personal account of my story thus far.

I hope I can bring you some peace and clarity about death and grief. I recently met a woman in a café who came over to me and thanked me for a blog post I wrote about dealing with loss at Christmas time. She said she always felt alone with grief but reading my piece made her realise that we all feel the same loss. That is my aim for this book, to show you that you are not alone on this journey.

'Broken Love' takes a look at the emotions tied to loss and grief. I lost my brother, Marcus, in 2005 in a car accident and my Dad, Maxie, passed away just a year later in 2006 after an illness. I was fifteen and sixteen years old at the time and those deaths shook me to the core and left me broken hearted. Since then, I have spent years working on myself as I travelled the dark road of grief. I've learned so much about it and learned to live with loss.

I also touch on separation and divorce, which is something I experienced as my parents broke up in 1993. Parents splitting up also brings with it loss and grief. I've also talked openly about the affect my grief had on those around me.

There's some poetry in here as well, stuff I've written over the years, very raw and honest accounts of what I was feeling at different times. I went through a lot of therapy down through the years and tried various healing methods all of which I mention and explore in this book. I am not a therapist nor have I ever formally studied psychology. I use personal stories to explain what I went through in the hope of shining light on the darkness and to assist you on your road to acceptance.

Thank you for reading and, remember, you never walk alone. Meghann.

SECTION I

BROKEN LOVE

My mind is restless yet my body stiff,
Thoughts running like wildfire spreading through a forest,
Yet my legs are stuck firmly to the ground.

I want to run, run from this place,
Get away from all this heartache,
But I'm stuck.

My mind is frantic with emotion
Like a startled animal filled with fear.

And my heart?
What heart?
What is even left of it?
Just shattered dreams and broken love,

If love is endless then why does it feel like this?

THE NIGHT MARCUS DIED

It was Friday the 4th of March and I came home close to 5pm from Seamount College in Kinvara having completed my Junior Cert mock exams. Marcus was the only one at home as I came through the back door. He had finished his Leaving Cert mocks on the Wednesday from Garbally College in Ballinasloe. He was getting his clothes ready for that night out in Galway and he also had his rugby gear ready. He always left a yellow box of sports gear inside the door of the kitchen. An unusual place for them, but that is where they stayed as he pulled fresh gear from them at the weekends.

A while later the phone rang and it was our neighbour, Cathal. We had a quick chat before I handed the phone to Marcus. They were arranging rugby training. Mam came home and we all had dinner at the house. She was a vegetarian at the time and Marcus always liked steak on a  Friday evening while I only ate chicken. So she made up three different dinners for us.

Later Mam dropped Marcus up to Cathal's house where the two set off for rugby training in Gort. In the meantime, I got ready to go horse riding. I was with the South Galway Pony Club at the time and we would have show jumping lessons on Friday nights behind Cummin's Kitchens on the Limerick road. It was halfway between Ardrahan and Gort. Dad was late so I went to the village to meet him. When he arrived and I got into the lorry I noticed numerous clothes stained with blood. I looked at him and the side of his head was split open. He'd had difficulty loading the horse and ended up hitting his head in the process. He was clearly in pain but as he was teaching the class he was determined to make it.

When we arrived into the yard and the parents saw him they refused to let him teach and sent him to the Doctor in Gort, someone drove him up. We kicked off with the class. After a while, I was standing in the corner of the arena with my friend, Nicola. We were waiting for our turn to jump the course. I was riding Dad's black stallion, King Cotton Gold. He was beautiful. Nicola and I laughed because he kept eyeing up her gelding (male) pony. I then noticed an ambulance heading towards Gort. It wasn't going very fast and the sirens weren't on but the blue lights flashed. I instantly panicked and thought something has happened to my Dad. I looked around the arena and saw him standing at the gate with his head bandaged. "Thank God," I uttered to myself. But After a while I spotted another ambulance travelling the Loughrea road towards Gort. I thought that was unusual.

I looked around the arena and spotted my Dad with a bandage on his head. While he was in the Doctor's surgery, the phone rang and the Doctor was called away as there had been an accident and he was needed. He told Dad to take his time and he went to the scene. Dad was driving back to me when he came upon the crash that his Doctor had been called to. The driver asked Dad should they stop and help but Dad said to stay driving, as they didn't want to cause another accident clogging the road.

After the lesson, Dad dropped me home. As soon as I walked in home Mam was flustered. Marcus' brand new black French Connection shirt lay on the ironing board, which was in the middle of the kitchen floor. Mam only ever ironed his shirts. She kept saying, "He should be home by now, he said 9 o'clock." It was roughly 9.10 and I reassured her that he was probably talking to the lads. He was only home weekends from boarding school. But something was up with her. She was unsettled. Eventually, she called the neighbours and they told her there had been a crash. She immediately fell to the floor in the back hall. I pulled her up and asked her who, but she hadn't been told so I was convinced it wasn't the boys but perhaps they had been caught in traffic due to the accident.

We went to granny's house and Mam told her that there had been a crash. She walked up the hall and she went to ground. I pulled her up too and told them all to stop jumping to conclusions. I was getting annoyed at them both for thinking the worst. I ran out to see where my uncle was and met him walking up granny's driveway. He drove Mam and I to the neighbour's house.

While standing in their driveway, the local GP arrived and was bringing the awful news that Cathal was dead. We were numb. He was my friend too and I was devastated for the family. While we stood in their front garden, which is on the main Galway road, an ambulance flew by. Little did we know that it was our beloved Marcus.

My uncle Peter drove Mam and I to the hospital. We stopped in a petrol station in Oranmore on the way and I got Mars Bars for Marcus. They were his favourite and I knew he would appreciate them in hospital. That drive in was rather calm as we tried to all talk about the future. Marcus may need to do the Leaving Cert the following year instead because he would be heartbroken over the passing of Cathal. We also noted that he would never cope if he was unable to play rugby for a few months if he was injured.

When we arrived to A&E I recognised loads of people. Friends from home, neighbours and family friends. I remember thinking this is random that so many I know are in here on the same night. Dad had gotten to the hospital before us and he was in some other room. Mam and I joined him and they were both asking for Marcus. I felt like I was in an episode of ER, a show I watched every Sunday night.

Eventually, a nurse pointed to double doors and said he was in there and I looked and they read 'Resuscitation Room'. That's odd, I thought. Why would he be in there?

We were placed in a small private room opposite and in here Mam became very agitated. I was telling her to calm down. Dad was in business mode wanting to chat to Doctors. I was still confused. Mam's friend, Máire, came into the room and brought a man with her who was dressed as a priest. I didn't know why she would bring a man we didn't know into the room. After what seemed like forever a nurse came back to talk to us and explain some injuries. It sounded a little more than a sprained ankle and concussion and we were told he was going to surgery and that the next two hours were crucial. Mam demanded we see him.

We were taken into that room with the double doors. It was a large ward but only one bed, where Marcus lay. Mam and Dad ran to his head and the nurse said, "mind the tubes, they are his lifeline." Again, I was thinking, what is she on about, that this woman must have thought we were in the latest ER episode making everything sound much more dramatic than it really was. But then Marcus moved his head and his eyes opened for a split second. "He's awake," I said.

"No," said the nurse. "That's the tube in his neck causing him to move."

Mam and Dad were crying. Mam kept telling him how much she loved him. Dad kept telling him to fight. Eventually, I went up to him and whispered in his ear. I bent down to him and said, "I got you Mars Bars for later," and then we left the room. We all went to the waiting room and I started watching the clock, two more hours and we could get to see him.

At this stage I knew everyone in the hospital around me and more arrived as the night wore on. I still didn't understand that they were all here for Marcus. Every fifteen minutes I would do a countdown of the time left in surgery. At this stage, those who weren't connected to us knew what was happening so the entire room waited with anticipation. My mother, in the meantime, found it too difficult seeing all the familiar faces. She had more of an understanding of the seriousness of Marcus' injuries. She, along with my Dad and a few family members, went to the second floor of the hospital where the surgery was taking place.

1.30 a.m. struck and I started to feel almost excited because we had only a half hour left. Then my aunt came from upstairs. She had a soft smile on her face as she walked into the waiting room. Everyone looked up at her and she came to me and asked me to come with her. He's awake, I thought to myself.

We walked up the corridor and she was holding my hand and patting it. "Is he awake?" I asked. She wasn't sure but was just told to come and get me. We walked into a large empty ward with loads of empty beds. I remember thinking this was unusual as the hospitals were always in the news for bed shortages. Dad was actually lying in one bed because he had split his head open earlier that day.

The surgeon came in with a nurse and Mam, Dad and I stood together. They started talking medical gibberish and were listing his endless injuries that I won't mention as it is quite upsetting to hear. As they spoke I stood waiting for the line that they always said in ER on Sunday nights, "But we managed to save him."

And I waited. Until eventually the surgeon said the line that I can hear still to this day.

"We did everything we could, we couldn't save him."

....

I looked at him very confused. They didn't say that in ER.

Mam collapsed to the floor wailing. Dad tried to pull her up. My family members all roared crying. Mam and Dad grabbed me. Everyone started pulling at me.

GO AWAY, I screamed in silence. I didn't want anyone to touch me. I was in a state of complete shock and denial. He is not dead. Marcus is not dead. My brother is not dead.

I later heard that one of my aunts walked downstairs to the waiting room that had become overcrowded with people we knew anxiously awaiting news about Marcus. She walked into the room and just shook her head. They knew.

Mam wanted to see him straight away so we were told that they would get him ready for us. We were taken to another ward on a different floor. Mam, Dad and I were shown to a private room where Marcus lay.

He looked sound asleep. Still colour in his cheeks, still handsome and so peaceful looking. I couldn't understand why he didn't wake.

We all spoke to him that night and we let everyone up to see him. News spread very fast throughout and even more people arrived in the early hours. Around 4 a.m., we all started to head home. I'll never forget being stuck in the car park because we didn't have change. Imagine, just seeing your brother dead in a hospital bed and consoling your mother, and not being able to leave the hospital grounds easily. Mam's friend, Máire, dropped us home after 4 a.m. I went straight to his room. Everything as perfect as always, the way he liked it. We managed to get to bed but by 6 a.m. Mam was walking around the house roaring crying. She went next door to granny's house and got into bed with her. My aunt Imelda was also there and they put Mam in the middle of the bed and held her.

That next morning I was numb. At the age of fifteen I had been through an extremely traumatic ordeal and my brother Marcus was dead. I never said goodbye to him that night and I still had his Mars Bars.

Over the next few days the house was awash with people who came to share their condolences. It was the most surreal experience. I had to talk to people I didn't even know. People hugged me and I hated it and perhaps that is why I now don't like being hugged. We held his funeral and gave him the most magical send off. I never thought a funeral could be described as a thing of beauty but in that church that day we all felt surrounded by love and care. We played Robbie Williams' song, 'Angels' during mass and as we carried him outside. That was the last CD I ever bought for him. Every time I hear that song I think of him. I read his eulogy that day and everyone was involved in his final journey. All his friends took turns carrying his body to its place of rest. Also, there was a butterfly flying around the sacristy during mass and we heard after that there was another one in the gallery resting on Cathal's uncle's shoulder.

The 5th of March, a day that would change my life forever.

Dear Marcus
(Written for his first anniversary mass)

A year gone by,
It's hard to believe,
It's been so long,
Since you were here with me.

On the 5th of March
God took you away,
It really broke my heart,
What more is there to say?

I think of you everyday
Growing up together
We had so much fun,
Memories I will treasure forever.

And when I cry,
I wonder why?
Why were you taken away?
Why couldn't you stay?

Now you're in heaven
An angel above
Looking down on us,
Sending your love.

I miss you so much,
Our hearts will never mend,
Until we meet again,
Goodbye my brother, goodbye my friend.

THE NIGHT DAD DIED

I have some very vivid memories from my childhood in Dublin. We only lived in Dundrum until I was five years old but I can remember some moments better than others. Lynwood is where I first learned to ride a bike without stabilizers. I made a snowman and refused to wear my gloves, which resulted in me sitting with my hands in a bowl of warm water. I remember catching my finger in the dining room door. In the garden I let our fluffy white rabbit out of the cage and watched as our Shih Tzu, Fuschia, killed him. All monumental moments.

I was just over two years old and it was late at night. I woke because there was a commotion downstairs. I walked down and saw my Mam at the kitchen door crying. Marcus was at the bottom of the stairs. Two men in bright yellow jackets were in the hallway and Dad was lying down on a bed with wheels. He had a heart attack and was being taken away in an ambulance. That is my first of many memories of him being seriously ill.

In 1995 we had just moved to Spiddal as my parents had separated. In April of that year my father went for a triple heart bypass and we were called back to Dublin. We were told to prepare for the worst. This was major heart surgery and rather invasive. I remember walking the

hospital hallway and knowing that the family were very bothered. By May he was able to attend Marcus' Communion Day but he wasn't in good shape. We have photos from that day and in one of them Dad is having medical complications and it is visible. He left early. From then on he was always in and out of hospitals and took numerous tablets every morning. It just became a part of life for him.

Every year in August, Dad and I would go to the RDS Horse Show in Dublin. We would travel up on the Sunday to get the best space in the Old Belvedere Rugby Club. The show didn't start until Wednesday. One year, I was about twelve, we went on up and he fell ill. A friend of a friend had a house around the corner and we went to stay with her because Dad must have known he was too unwell for just me to mind him. I stayed in this house while he went to the hospital. But he was a fighter and the horse show was his favourite time of year so he made sure he was in the main arena by Wednesday morning. That week, I was always keeping an eye on him because I knew it was his stubborn nature keeping him on that showground and not his health.

Another year, when I was 14, I brought two school friends to the horse show with me. We settled into our usual spot there. As we were going year after year, we got to know so many people and Dad was well known in the horse world. The first night he was up coughing nonstop. He kept us all awake, I checked on him but he swore he was fine. Eventually, at dusk he got up and said to me he would be back soon. A guy in a lorry beside us drove him to hospital. I watched as he drove off and he told me not to worry. He was kept in that night and I was riddled with fear. Firstly, we were all alone in the lorry, three teenage girls, and I knew Dad was not well but once show day came, he was back.

Maxie Scully was like the bionic man. It seemed that nothing could kill him. He took on every illness and bet it. He was a fighter. It was admirable the way he got knocked down and picked himself back up every time. He always had goals that drove him on. He loved the horse show so much that he signed himself out of hospital just to be there and he would spend the entire five days at the show, morning until night. A fear of missing out perhaps, something I certainly have.

But in 2005, when tragedy struck and Marcus was taken from us, I saw Dad dwindle before my very eyes. The shock and pain was too much for him. He had spent fifty-two years battling illness after illness but never let it stop him living his life. Marcus was eighteen and he had his whole life ahead of him. It was cruel.

After Marcus' death, Dad went to South Africa for an extended period. I thought he initially went for a holiday but weeks soon turned into months. While over there, he had some more health complications and ended up in hospital. I'm not fully aware of what happened but when he returned in November he wasn't the same man that left me. We had plans to take the horse show jumping all around Ireland and I was going to spend months getting stronger and improving at horse riding. His health had deteriorated and he seemed to have lost his spark. I never asked him about that trip because he seemed shaken from it and my aim was to get him better. The only thing he did say to me was that South Africa was the closest thing to paradise he had ever seen and that one day we would go together.

He dipped in and out of hospital for the coming weeks and in January he went in for longer periods. Marcus' first anniversary took place on the 5th of March 2006 and Dad was in hospital. But he always left for events over the years so we waited for him to arrive. Even when the mass began I looked around for him. Surely, he would never miss this day. But he did. And then I knew that this was very serious.

He came out of hospital briefly but it was only for a few days here and there. I realised when I spent time with him that he wasn't himself. In June of 2006, he was due for a hospital appointment in Dublin and he booked us onto the breakfast train from Galway. I was incredibly nervous because I knew his health was deteriorating and he wasn't at all well. I think he noticed that I was being overly cautious, making sure he sat down and keeping my hands out as he sat and stood. The train up was lovely, we got breakfast and he recalled going on the same journey with his father, Mark, 'back in the day.' When we got to Dublin he wanted me to go shopping. We took the Luas, both for the first time, to Jervis Street. We went into the newly opened Jervis Street shopping centre and he showed me where the ward was that he got his kidney transplant back in 1975. I couldn't believe that this place, now full of lovely new clothes shops, was where my Dad had a serious operation when he was twenty-one.

I went to the bathroom and when I came out there was no sign of him. I became panicked as I waited because I knew he was a very ill man. I watched men come in and come out and I was about to go in looking when he appeared. He wasn't his usual strong self and he walked very slowly. He insisted we went shopping but I didn't want to, as I was apprehensive. We went to Penney's for a look and I have to say that trip warmed my heart. Dad was wearing his Stetson hat, not for fashion but because he has an open wound on his temple and it was covered with a large white bandage. He didn't want people seeing it so the hat helped, although you could still see it. The security man in Penney's saw him and straight away offered him a chair and then he sent me off shopping. I had no interest but I knew he wanted to buy me something. I spotted these black kitten heels but they weren't in my size. He asked a shop assistant and she went off and found a pair in the back. She even took the cash from Dad and went off and did the transaction for us leaving Dad sitting. That warmed my heart and I still have those shoes.

That trip meant so much to me as it was one of the last we would take together and alone. I was a Daddy's girl and loved spending time with him, but I never realised that trip on the train would be our last together. After that he went back in to hospital one last time. When I went to see him there he was acting very unusual. I used to go in alone to him and was never made aware of what medications he was on. I expected to come into the room and chat to my Dad about school, horses and the usual musings a parent and child would have. The medication and health complications meant that wasn't the person I met when I walked through the door. He would be in the room with me chatting normally and then his eyes would change and he would tell me to look at horses. One day I ran out of the room and ran straight out the hospital doors because I was so scared. I didn't know what was going on. It was truly frightening to watch the man I loved, my protector, dwindle and fade before my eyes. After that, I had more of an idea that he was hallucinating so when he spoke of the lovely dog he could see by his bed, I agreed. I didn't want to confuse or stress him.

Day by day his health faded. Once August arrived, we knew that there wasn't long left with Dad. But I thought that he might just pull through because the horse show was coming and he loved it. He had a lot of visitors coming in to see him, which I didn't like. He needed to conserve his energy. As faces came and went he was asking for my mother but she was not let in to see him. It was devastating and one regret I hold on to. I wish I were stronger and stood up to those who blocked the door and wouldn't let her in. He had told his friends that he wanted to say sorry to her. He never got that chance. He wanted to say sorry that the marriage never worked out, something I talk about in more detail in the Separation and Divorce chapter. I guess what he really wanted was to say goodbye to her. She was after all his only wife.

For me, it would have been a very special moment because the death of Marcus left hurt between them both. His death left a hole in their lives. They brought him into this world. He was who he was because of them. And Dad was going to be reunited with Marcus first, and we both knew that Marcus was ready and waiting for him. I believe in heaven and I know that Marcus was the first person to walk Dad through those gates. No matter what, the four of us are family and nobody can ever take that away. We were a unit but we were separated on earth. We never got to say goodbye to Marcus but now we had a chance to say goodbye to Dad, and Mam should have been there to do that. Dying and death should be peaceful, loving, caring and all about family but it can bring people to dark places, to say nasty things and to do unusual things. I have forgiven the people that stopped my Mother coming in to see my Dad because life is too short, and for me to hold onto that anger will only cause me more pain and won't help me to heal.

On the 7th of August things took a turn for the worst. He was still talking but sleeping more. He couldn't eat and I tried to give him his sugary tea. The next day, he couldn't drink properly so I dipped these sponges into the tea and placed them in his mouth. It was heart-breaking having to sponge feed my own Dad. I would look into his eyes and try to keep smiling to make him feel at ease. He was sleeping a lot more now and wasn't saying much, but one day he woke and the last words he uttered were, "Diamonds for Meghann."

I went home every night but came back in every day. And each time, I watched him fade away. I asked for him to be tubed but was told I wasn't a Doctor. It made no sense to me. It felt like nobody was doing anything to help or save him. I still believed then that he could pull through and I wasn't ever willing to give up hope.

On the 11th of August I decided I was staying the night. He was just sleeping most of the time. I loved sitting beside him and he wore a gold ring that was a horse's head set in diamonds. I would sit and hold his hand and rub his ring. That ring was his pride and joy. Those few days in the hospital were draining. So many people came and went and, at one stage, I could hear talk of which readings should be chosen for his funeral. I was so angry. He was still alive. He could hear everything. If I could turn back time I would have kicked everyone out and just left him and I there for those final days.

That night a lovely nurse who knew Dad very well was on duty. She got me a bed in the ward to rest my head. Around 2 a.m. she ran down and called us in. His time had come. I was at his side holding his hand. I was telling him how much I loved him and that Marcus was waiting for him. I thought dying would be a peaceful experience but there were a number of us in that room. I just zoned in on my Dad and tried to block everyone else out. I watched as he took his final breath. It was surreal. One moment he was breathing and the next he wasn't.

I got home around 4 a.m. and again the numbness took over. Mam opened the door to me and I just said, "He's gone" and went to bed. The next day I sat in the living room and I felt so empty. The first man I ever loved was gone and I would never see him alive again. I had no brother and no father.

His funeral came and went and he was cremated in Glasnevin cemetery. He always planned on being cremated whereas Marcus was buried. I didn't get his ashes. I remember the first Christmas after his passing and, as the ashes hadn't been scattered, I wanted them, but was refused which added to my already broken heart. After months, my Dad's ashes were scattered along the fields of Ardrahan as we all went on horseback jumping walls. Funerals are horrible and very tough. I would ask that if children are involved that they are made the priority during these sad times. I was very much involved in every aspect of Marcus' funeral because I was his little sister and I knew what he wanted. As for Dad's funeral, I felt very much in the background and I felt I didn't get to give him the send-off that I gave Marcus. I was his number one and his little girl but it didn't feel like that on the day. Even as I write this and relive that time, I cannot help but cry and I can still feel the pain and loneliness. Never underestimate the feelings of a young boy or girl. It doesn't matter what age we are, we still feel the same loss and the same hurt. We have also lost the person we love.

The one thing that I took away from his death was that he died during the RDS Horse Show. He couldn't attend that year but when he passed, a minute's silence was held for him and that would have made him so proud. He died between his two favourite competitions, the Aga Khan and the Puissance. I still go to the RDS and I really feel connected to him when I am there. I once went back to the Old Belvedere Rugby Grounds to see all the lorries lined up but it just felt weird not seeing the maroon and white Oakley Bedford at the entrance gate. That lorry became a haven for all the pony riders. It was the place we all hung out together and got to know each other. It was truly a magical time.

Marcus' death was a shock, a tragedy, and unexpected, while Dad was dying for most of my life. I wasn't with Marcus when he died but I held Dad's hand when he passed away. Both affected me in different ways, which I aim to explain throughout this book.

Dear Dad
(Written on the 12th of August, 2006)

As I watched you pass away,
There was so much I wanted to say,
And the pain grew I my heart
Because the time had come to part.

It hurts to say goodbye
To someone I love so much,
But I've got the memories
That I will always clutch.

Your passion for horses,
Your eye for the courses,
The greatest horseman I ever met
And known so well for the record you set.

The tears will flow
As time passes by slow,
But you'll suffer no more
As you pass through heaven's door.

Now you're with Marcus
In the land above,
Together forever,
Sending your guidance, your love.

I'll think of you everyday
And miss you so much,
But you'll be in my heart's core
Forevermore.

Separation and Divorce

First and foremost, I love my father very much but he had his faults. And if he were here he would you tell you himself that he was the reason for the breakdown of the marriage.

Parents' separating is incomprehensible as a child because it is their job as your first teacher to teach you love, respect and care. We, as children look at how our parents treat each other and this can have a profound effect on our later relationships.

This might sound bizarre, but on reflection, I am glad Mam and Dad didn't stay together. It was an unhealthy relationship that would have caused us all greater upset in life. I commend my mother for having the strength not to let Dad come back.

Realising this fact was a revelation for me and one I discovered at a young age. As mentioned above, Dad was the reason behind the break up and he wasn't an easy man to live with. My brother and I had to be in bed by the time he came home from work and if we were awake, dare we speak. He had an old school way about him; children should be seen and not heard. He expected his dinner at a certain time every day and it had to be dished the way he liked it.

He was a strict father that demanded respect through fear. Not that he ever hit me but he had this power to control. I was petrified of him, and as a young child I felt this man was part of my life but not necessarily my father. As in, he didn't play with us as children. We had our own separate playroom and that was where we stayed, while he lived with us.

I did say I that I have utmost respect for my mother because although she was under his control as well, she knew we couldn't grow in this environment. I have to add that in time my relationship and life with my Dad grew and we became a strong unit.

In this chapter, I aim to help you to understand what it is like to be the child in the middle of a separation; living though the arguments, being the football kicked between the two, and moving on with the change.

The Break Down

My Dad was a character; he loved many things in life, horses, Bacardi, Carroll's cigarettes, and the high life. When he married my mother he quit almost all of these things but he had an addictive personality. He slowly returned to every single one of them. I won't talk about what he did as he isn't here anymore and it isn't fair on my mother, but he let her down. There is one thing I will say and that is the fact that he only ever loved my mother and no other woman came close to her. Even on his deathbed, his final wish was to say sorry to her, something he never got to do.

The Arguments

I have to note that I was only three or four years old when my parents' marriage began to dissolve, but I can remember the fighting as clear as day. I can recall it was Easter time and Marcus and I were in our playroom, we listened to the screaming next door. We decided to interrupt to show Dad the chocolate eggs we received. He didn't even look and ordered us out of the room. That was a common theme during those years we lived in Dublin.

I recall we had a little toilet under the stairs and each time Dad stormed out following another fight, I would go to this bathroom, get a tissue and take it to Mam because she was always left crying.

Even as small children we are aware of right and wrong, happiness and sadness. Oftentimes, the adults forget this and think children don't know that we'll forget. We don't. I was a toddler and I can remember all of the fights and arguments clearly, the fear and sadness that lay over our house.

The Moving

I remember the day my Dad moved out of our house. He had a maroon and white horse box and I helped him carry his belongings out. My mother stood at the front door upset. It was all she seemed to do those days. I felt so useful as I carried his belongings to the horsebox. My Dad needed my help and for once wasn't asking me to go inside.

This wasn't to be the end of moving for me. You see, the fallout of break ups can be immense. Money becomes the main issue. We were living in a large three story house in the suburbs of South Dublin. It contained the best furniture and paintings. It was Mam and Dad's dream home. He had a successful business and she was the perfect housewife. But with the separation came financial struggles. I'm no longer afraid to admit it, but we couldn't afford the house anymore.

The For Sale sign soon followed and every day we came back from school the wind seemed to have knocked that intrusive sign over. It turned out it was my mother trying to stall us losing our home so suddenly. But it was inevitable.

We had to up and move and at that time my mother was young, single and had two children. She felt she had failed and didn't want to return to her hometown. We got an invite to Spiddal in Connemara and we took it. Marcus and I went to a school in Dublin that taught hundreds of children, it was modern and in the suburbs. We had our three-storey house and the finest furniture. From that, we moved into a rented bungalow, leaving most of our possessions behind us, as we simply hadn't the space.

For Marcus, he struggled in the new surroundings. Spiddal was a beach town in a bog land, Irish-speaking area, and there was no soccer just Gaelic football. He was certainly a city slicker and the lack of a male presence to guide him affected him greatly. He got into trouble almost every day in school. He was hot headed and difficult. I almost feel he was sensitive and harbouring a lot of anger. He suddenly had to become the man of the house, the protector at a very young age.

Me on the other hand, I adored my new life by the beach. I settled in extremely easily. I was always much better at hiding my pain and I had a very relaxed attitude. I just wanted to play and be happy. But I always knew that I was different. It was the early '90's in Ireland, not many families were broken up. But in Spiddal, we were welcomed with open arms and people genuinely cared for us.

We were living in rented houses, so we eventually built our own bungalow in Ardrahan, a small village in South Galway where my mother is from. Again, I just slotted in in Ardrahan also. Marcus had started boarding school in Garbally at this stage, so he was finding his way.

For me, moving from place to place is just my way of life. I enjoy it. I'm not sure I will ever settle in one place. Home for me is a different word. Home isn't where my house is; it's where my heart, mind, body and soul are. When people ask me where I am from I reply by saying "Ardrahan and Spiddal" because Ardrahan is where my mother is but Spiddal is my spiritual home. My years spent there were carefree. I could be a new person, and nothing traumatic ever happened us when we were by the sea.

Moving can be so detrimental on young people especially after the breakup of a marriage but it can also be a time of discovery. You need to grab it with both hands and go on a journey. I've made friends in every place I have lived, I've found new hobbies and everything has inevitably led to the life I now live.

New Relationships

If you ask anyone whose parents broke up whom they least like when their parents are dating, it will be the new partner that has been brought into their home. My mother was always extremely careful with whom she dated and introduced to us. Marcus was a little more difficult with them whereas I was the accepting one. Once Mam was happy I was happy. Marcus gave every man a hard time in the beginning. But I have to say, they treated him like he needed to be treated, a young boy. Taking him to training and matches, brought outside to practice, the simple things Dad never did with him.

My father, on the other hand, introduced us to some horrible, nasty women. For some reason he was attracted to some very difficult people, ones that turned on us. This caused massive problems in our young lives. One woman he dated we nicknamed Poison. She was dangerous. We often had to spend holidays with Dad as per court documents and Mam never wanted us to be apart from him. She felt it was important we knew our father. When we first met Poison she lived near Dublin, and often when my father left for work she would lock us outside of the house until it came time for him to return home. She would then load us with chocolate and sugar to almost make us forget the past few hours outdoors.

She really clashed with Marcus, as she knew his relationship was fractured with Dad. She would often take me shopping and buy me nice things and nothing for Marcus. As a small girl, I never understood, I was just so happy with my toy kitchen and pretty dresses.

I guess a pivotal point came when Marcus, Dad and I were spending a day together. When we returned to our room, Marcus noticed something wasn't right with his bag of clothes. While we were away she spilt bleach all over his clothes and destroyed them. I will never forget the sadness on Marcus' face because of what she had done.

Her and Dad's relationship was toxic. Like nothing I have ever seen before, and she, a grown woman, took this out on Marcus and I, children. After years, when Dad eventually left her, it seemed the sun was shining again but she had already caused the hurt and the trauma remained. She damaged the relationship between Dad and Marcus almost beyond repair. Marcus refused to spend time with Dad because of her, and for some years they barely spoke.

Parents are entitled to new relationships but they must also consider what influences they are bringing into their children's lives. Equally, children can sometimes be difficult with new men and women but this has to be taken into consideration as well.

Divorce

My parents were only ever separated. As the years rolled on my Mam thought it best they get a divorce but it wasn't happening. She never pushed for one but they used to joke about it. They did become friends in time and had a laugh together. Dad even befriended her partner as well.

The whole divorce idea was never at the fore, in fact it was only really mentioned in passing. After Marcus died they even considered getting back together through sheer devastation. Dad though got quite sick after Marcus' death and once he darkened the doors of the hospital that was the end for him. I did mention before that his final wish was to say sorry to Mam, which something he never got to do as my mother was not let into the room because he signed the divorce papers before he died. He said it was a dying wish to her, but in actual fact it caused more harm.

Being divorced meant she was not his next of kin; I was under eighteen so it fell on someone else. Therefore my mother had zero rights anymore. It is something that when I think of it upsets me, but I have to let that go too. He did what he thought was right for her without thinking of the consequences.

Understanding

Divorce is a tricky situation. It is the end of the marriage, and in so many ways it's the end of an era, a lifetime. Suddenly, a once madly in love couple are now strangers, effectively.

We as children need to also respect our parents' loss and pain. While it is never easy on us being dragged through every fight, mentally and verbally, we must take a step away. We need to protect ourselves but also care for the people that brought us into this world.

But Only For A While

Death is pain
But only for a while.
Death is sadness
But only for a while.
Death is depression
But only for a while.
Death is shock
But only for a while.
Death is fear
But only for a while.
Death is anger
But only for a while.
Death brings acceptance
Acceptance lasts forever.

LIVING WITH GRIEF

PART 1

My journey with grief began after losing my brother and my father during my teenage years, 2005 and 2006. But I found it wasn't until 2011 when I started to really evolve through the stages of grief as I began writing every single day because I didn't know how else to express my pain and loss. It became a relief and a safe haven to share my thoughts and feelings. It gave me the confidence to open up to those around me.

One summer I was living with my friends in Galway city and I was on the dole having just finished my Master's Degree, I felt completely lost and mentally unable to do any work. I just took some time off to sort myself out which I feel is very important and something I will explain further on (Me Day).

The girls all worked and during the day and while they were gone, I had the house to myself. I would clean the place, light some candles and just read and write. Some days I would read back over old entries to show myself how far I had come. These diaries became very important to me and to my learning and growing through loss and grief. I brought a diary everywhere, always in my handbag because sometimes I would get an urge to write, be it on a bus, in the park or sitting having a coffee.

When life is good my pen won't write, yet when my mind is full the words fall onto the page like autumn leaves falling from a tree.

I wrote this poem at a time when I was very sad and when I was feeling a little unsure, but that's what living with grief is like. People talk about living with disease and sometimes the emotions around someone dying can seem like an incurable illness yet if we dig deep we can find a cure.

I'm still working through it and each day it gets better, sometimes I still suffer a setback, and that's normal. That's life.

It's to honour and cherish those we have lost and believe that no matter what they are that driving force behind us, that they are in fact the cure.

I lost my brother Marcus in 2005. He was eighteen years old at the time when he lost his young life in a car accident. He was my older brother, just two and a half years between us. At the time, I was a child and felt I couldn't grieve, so I made it my own business to be strong for my family and to hide my tears in my pillow.

And only a year and a half later my father, Maxie, lost his battle with illness. While Doctors say it was illness, I believe it was grief that killed him. I was always very close to my father. I shared his love for horses and every weekend we headed off to shows together. When I lost him, I wasn't sure if I would ever be able to pick up the broken pieces of my heart. Horse riding was the first thing that slipped away. And even now I still feel extremely sad when I'm galloping through a field. I could be surrounded by sixty people preparing to jump walls, and yet I feel so lonely because this is a place where I should be with my Dad. We had plans for me to progress in show jumping and he was handing over the reins, literally. When filling out the show jumping papers it was my name that Dad put down as the rider. A dream neither of us got to see. I say that I will someday return to horses on a more full time basis, but right now is not the right time.

Losing the first two men you learn to love is devastating and incomprehensible. I was a child and I was suddenly thrown into this world of darkness, pain and despair.

Every day for a number of years I woke up feeling completely empty, like there wasn't much reason to get out from under the duvet. Some days, I would look at the window and just see dark clouds. I would always find a reason to stay indoors, to hide from the world.

When I went out panic and dread would overcome me, so much so that when I was in the city I avoided the main streets and took back roads for fear of seeing anyone I knew.

I didn't have the interest for makeup or dressing nicely, but wouldn't want anyone to see me dishevelled. Some days I would force myself to change into something nice and put on some makeup but doing so just felt like I was putting a mask on, masking the feelings and struggling to smile.

Writing though offered me a platform to learn, heal and discover, and now I can share my experience to help you in some way.

The first ever post I shared about what I was suffering was 'This Is Me', which explains some of my journey.

Here is a poem I wrote describing my grief:

Grief
The glass is empty yet heavy,
The eyes are open yet empty,
The heart is beating yet cold,
The heart is pumping yet broken.
Moving forward yet stuck in the past,
Living today but dreaming of yesterday,
Wanting to move yet my feet are stuck,
Want to be set free but I'm trapped inside.
Needing love yet pushing it away,
Wanting care yet staying alone,
Asking for help yet never listening,
Praying for shelter but staying outdoors.

LIVING WITH GRIEF

PART 2

When it comes to sharing a personal message I sometimes hesitate. Even writing this book, putting my personal life onto pages for all to see and read. What will people think? Will they think I am mad? Attention seeking? Here she goes again? I tremble with the thought of people talking about me negatively, but then I reassure myself that a

problem shared is a problem halved. And being able to at least open up about it and talk about it gets the conversation going, and in ways, a domino effect is created. For so many years following the passing of Marcus and Dad I put on a big smile and a brave face. When it eventually caught up with me in 2011 I thought that nobody would believe me that I was grieving, especially so many years later. It was still a short space of time, 5-6 years, but I didn't understand that either. I once read in a book that grief takes five years to reach the stage of acceptance, and I naively believed this to be a fact. For months, I genuinely believed that I was losing my mind. At the point of no return.

I struggle to talk openly about, well, my struggle. My way of opening up is to write. Maybe I hide behind my computer sometimes but isn't this better than keeping it locked inside a heavy heart? That is how I felt when I shared my very first blog post 'This Is Me'. I couldn't tell people in person what I was feeling or going through but technology gave me that platform. When people then approached me about it I was able to share more of my life, my pain and my anguish. I didn't have to pretend any more or put on this show. The happy, lively, fun girl could show her flaws, her damaged wings and her dented spirit. Anyway I was exhausted from putting on a show. I wasn't going to be able to keep it up for much longer.

You see, I write a lot about grief and how to get through it yet I forget to look after myself. For a while, I didn't practice what I preach and while others thanked me for my words of wisdom, I cowered in a corner trying to keep it all in.

Many well-known figures have opened up in recent years about the struggles facing youth today, how depression is becoming an epidemic. We see it being heavily discussed among millennials across social media platforms. It is being spoken about in the Dáil (Irish government). More newspapers and online websites are dedicating pages to wellness and mental health. I am part of the series of books called 'Mental Health For Millennials' where so many people with different professions and lives have opened up about their personal and professional experiences. It's so great and refreshing to see. I've listened to Blindboy Boatclub of the Rubberbandits open up so honestly about mental health and his clear and concise approach has a real can-do-can talk attitude.

For me, grieving was my epidemic. It worms its way into every sense, emotion and crevice and buries itself deep inside me only to expose itself when I least expect it. And sometimes, I feel we are hit with such tragedy in everyday life, that so many of us are grieving at the one time but never together. We feel so lonely and isolated.

I remember one Monday back in 2013, I was living in London at the time and had holidays to use up with work. It was October time and my birthday. I had a fun weekend celebrating with my friends but that day off it hit me. I planned a day out for myself and headed for Westfield's shopping Centre in Shepherds Bush. It has almost 400 stores and 4,500 parking spaces just to give you an idea of its enormity. And there I was feeling like desperately lonely. I even went to my favourite coffee spot, Pret, and ordered my usual, latte and a ham and cheese hot croissant. It was always my treat and even that couldn't make me smile. I bought a new diary that day and felt the tears coming to my eyes, so I started writing.

Here is that diary entry:

October 28th 2013

Sitting among the hustle and bustle of Westfield in Shepherds Bush – children laughing, mothers stressed, employees rushing to get a quick lunch. Then there is me. On annual leave and where better to spend the day but in shopping. The wind howling outside as a storm batters the UK.

Instead of enjoying this moment I am trying to control my breathing, holding back for fear the tears will resemble that of the storm outside.

The lunchtime rush in Pret meant time chosen wrongly by me sitting at a table with a complete stranger but that is London, strangers everywhere, from all corners of the globe, searching, seeking, running, hiding, frightened, nervous, and anxious. Or is that just me?

That is how my days felt in those years. I've often discussed the five stages of grief as written about by Elizabeth Kubler Ross: Denial, Anger, Bargaining, Depression and finally, Acceptance.

Some days I used to wake up and jump from my bed with an air of happiness and I would think it has finally happened, I had reached the point of acceptance. But the reality was I hadn't. It is many years since grief came knocking on my door yet some days I wake up and I feel like I am back in the hospital, the moment the surgeon came in to tell us Marcus did not survive, the words etched on my brain.

Those days I have felt that I'm further from acceptance than ever. Living with grief, for me, was at times like living with a disease. My Dad suffered with various health issues over the years and I saw firsthand with him what it was like. Some days he got up and made his own tea, other mornings I would have to take it to him. When I used to go to bed, I never knew how I would wake up. And I have tried the positive steps: reading and writing, meditation, and mindfulness to ensure a fresh mind going to sleep. I steer clear of watching Netflix too late and don't watch any dark series at nightfall. Because something as simple as a fictional show, all made up, could be a trigger. I remember watching a war movie. It was all loud noises, rifles and air strikes. That night I was transported into a war zone and when I woke up I felt anxious and out of sorts.

I've had to accept that there is no quick fix.

Grief takes time and a lot of tears.

It also brings with it anger, an anger that is like a ticking time bomb, triggered by something mundane – an ignored text, a day with no fresh air, a comment you read on social media – all can be triggers. It is important to recognize your triggers, make note of them and try avoiding them or working with them.

Another aspect of grief for me was feeling like I was a burden to people around me. When I had spells of feeling low and down in myself I thought people wouldn't want to be around me. I would try to avoid housemates by staying in my room, go for a drive in my car, or hideaway. I didn't understand there were people who wanted to help me and didn't mind when I wasn't in the best of form. Instead of accepting love, I avoided it.

Here is another diary entry I wrote about feeling like a burden:

*January 23*rd *2016*

For me, it is easier to keep people at arm's length because I never want to be a burden. Many people will offer themselves to a weakened soul but in reality, very few can be there when it strikes. Which is okay too. They have their own lives.

But sadly this has hardened my heart. I can't remember what it feels like to be embraced because I won't let anyone get that close to me. I'd love nothing more than to lie on a sofa for the day but I'm physically not able for that. Not right now.

As I type I've tears streaming down my face and I can't stop them so I'm just going to let them fall. I know this will pass. I just don't know when.

It is the weekend after all. But sometimes this happens when I have a busy day of meetings, work and errands to run but I've mastered the hide and slide technique.

Lots of concealer, large sunglasses and a fast-paced walk. Don't get me wrong, not every day is this bad. Some days are so much fun and productive with plans for world domination!
But sometimes, life has a habit of getting me down and there is only so much I can do. I try to lead a perfect life but maybe my imperfections are what makes me Me. Maybe grief is just who I am now. Maybe this is my life.

It happened to me for a reason.
Everything happens for a reason.

I've learned over the years that I am not burden to anyone. And I am not a burden to myself. It was a process that I went through, and with time and patience, I've learned to accept a helping hand from those people kind enough to offer it.

LIVING WITH GRIEF

PART 3

As mentioned in previous chapters, I always found writing to be such a strong aid in my journey through grief. It helps me to understand what I am going through, and seeing it on paper, raw and very real, shows me

that I am not losing my mind completely. I am on this journey and I am discovering who I am and what has happened to me.

As I write this piece, Galway have just won their first hurling All-Ireland in 29 years. Many people were asking why I was not going to attend but, to be honest, my last trip to Croke Park tells a very different story. Granted Galway lost, but there was more to it than that for me.

It was two years ago, I landed in Dublin from a sun holiday on Saturday. I even met Conor McGregor in the airport carrying yet another 'champs belt.' It was exciting and a great way to kick off the weekend. That night, I felt on edge but ignored my gut and decided to go partying with my fellow Galwegians.

Anxiety and alcohol are never a good mix. I ended up in the well-known nightclub, Coppers, and to be honest it went downhill from there. I arrived back to my house with no keys, phone or wallet. It might sound like an average wild night out but it was dangerous and irresponsible on my part. I should have seen the signs and stayed in that night but there has always been this fear of missing out with me. It's a common phrase we throw around playfully, but for me back then sitting at home in silence would make me think and feel about what was really going on in my head and my heart and that scared me. A night out seemed like the best distraction, dancing, music, friends and a place to forget about it all.

The next morning I had to find my family and make my way to Croke Park. I felt particularly down, feeling sorry for myself if anything, and trying to mask the pain by saying I had a hangover. My ticket was in the Cusack Stand and I was sitting on my own. The crowds and noise put me on edge. I felt this dark fear hang over me as I sat around 80,000 plus people. The excitement off them should have been enough to spurn me on and shake it off. But it didn't work. It was a momentous day for Galway hurling but I felt like I was from the opposite side of the world. I had no interest, I lost that spark and excitement that takes hold on All-Ireland day.
We lost that match, but I had lost long before that.

I got myself home that night and fell to pieces. A few things happened and it felt like the straw that broke the camel's back.

In the week that followed I quit my job. I felt hopeless, pathetic, useless and a nuisance. I moved home, back in with my mother.

I felt I had returned to an all too familiar dark place.

Not long after that, my Mam got me in the car and took me for a drive. The destination, Pieta House in Tuam. I went for an assessment and within days began a programme with them. I'm not saying I wanted to take my own life but I had become so low that I needed serious help. This feeling had been coming and going for quite a number of years at this stage. I had tried antidepressants but didn't want them again. I am aware that some people need them and talking to your local Doctor is advised. I had taken them but I just didn't want them as I felt they weren't healing me as such, only prolonging emotional damage that needed to be dealt with at some stage, sooner rather than later on my part.

As I sat in that waiting room week after week, I wasn't sure that I would find solace. But in that room with the counsellor it all unravelled. I finished my course and I was really upset leaving that final day, more so because it was time for me to go on my own and use the tools that had been shown to me in Pieta House.

Since that time I have built a life for myself using what I learned in Tuam. I've also gone for alternative healing as well and given myself little treats along the way. I've realised that going to counselling and asking for help is by no means embarrassing or needs to be such an alien concept.

In 2017, I found myself feeling low again but not wanting to return to a complete place of darkness, I went for therapy in Limerick City. It was an investment in myself. I went for just over eight weeks, one day a week to begin and then every fortnight. I finished before Christmas and felt it was just what I needed.

Sometimes we can get so caught up in everyday life, in social media and this ever-expanding world of technology that we lose sight of our mission. I used to read quite a lot but have struggled from time to time as I get engrossed in a Netflix series, but this year, I started reading again, every night, a few pages. Reading is wonderful, be it a novel, sci-fi, mindfulness or a good autobiography, whatever tickles your fancy.
It has by no means been an easy road but I've picked myself up and with the right support and love I've turned my life around. It's Version 2.0 of Meghann. And if I need to go on to version 3.0 then so be it, because now I know how to do it and I know there is someone out there that will listen, guide and help me.
I've found a job I love and a life I love.
I still take each day as it comes.
One day at a time.
I know that dark days will come, but they will go.
Because each day I am learning.
It's like sitting an exam, you study and you prepare so on the day you know you will pass because you've done the necessary work. You may get a trick question in there as well but it won't be so daunting.

COMING TO BETTER UNDERSTAND
ME AND GRIEF

I first explored Elisabeth Kubler Ross and the five stages of grief while studying for my Master's Degree back in 2012. I picked up her book 'On Grief and Grieving' in the NUIG library. As I read through her work, page by page, I felt a great sense of relief and my heavy heart lifted. For the first time in what felt like a lifetime, someone knew and understood *my* pain. It was as though I could hear someone sit beside me in the library and comfort me. It was a revelation, a eureka moment. I read

quotes such as *"The will to save a life is not the power to stop a death"* and *"Anger affirms that you can feel, that you did love and that you have lost,"*

I was sitting in the NUIG library and, as it was summertime, students, stressed out studying for repeats and thesis deadlines, visited the place. I'd say if anyone saw my face that day they must have felt a pang of jealousy perhaps thinking I had completed an essay or obtained an A in my exam. I was smiling and nodding to the pages before my eyes because it was such a momentous moment for me.

I can still remember that day fondly. And I say *fondly* because it was the road less travelled that I had taken, and it took me to this moment. It was a brief moment along that journey but one in which I spent time for I thought this was the end of the road. I had reached my goal, I accepted what had happened, Marcus had died and so had Dad. But this was not the end of the road. It was merely an early watering post, a place that told me to keep going, never give up. And that day the storm began to lift and the clouds dispersed. For a time.

Since then, I've continued along that path, a territory unexplored, unknown of, for that is my pathway, and this is my journey. I'm still on it and I am learning each and every day. You, too, are on your own journey and I am a post along that route to guide you, comfort you and tell you to keep going.

I've been writing for some years now and as I came to grips with the five stages of grief, I found there to be many sub categories. There are emotions I had never even dreamed of, unexposed, raw and challenging; areas that we will all encounter at some stage or another. I became interested in studying grief as a concept and construct. I went in search of literature that would help me but also teach me. Here are some of the other areas and stages of grief I have come to experience:

Anxiety:

I think almost all of us experience anxiety, be it mild forms or more extreme. I had bouts of anxiety throughout my life and while in University, but at that time I never understood what it really was.

I have a vivid memory from my childhood, roughly three years old. My parents were finalising their separation and our home life was being totally disrupted. I recall staying in a flat with a friend of my parents'. I think Marcus and I spent time in other people's homes while our parents tried to deal with their marriage woes and eventual parting. I remember being in this house but I did not feel safe. I was uneasy and I can remember that trapped feeling taking over, not really knowing my surroundings or those around me. They were friends of the family, but strangers to me.

My Dad and I went to the horse show every single year. It became our thing. I loved that week so much, spending quality time with my father or in reality being company for him and also minding our horse lorry. During those years show goers would park their lorries in the Old Belvedere Rugby Club grounds and it was like one great campsite. BBQ's, drinking, fun and games ensued every evening following a day of show jumping. It really was a place of security and freedom. This particular night, when I was 11 or 12 years old, I stayed with my friend in her lorry, which was a luxurious, brand new type. Once I lay down, this panic fell upon me and in the middle of the night I had to leave and return to my safe haven.

I had some more of these episodes growing up, but it was in college that they became more frequent. While studying for my undergrad in the University of Limerick, I had a few unmanageable moments. One night, anxiety fell over my every being. I couldn't sit with it. I was alone at the time in my room and instead of going to my housemates, I opened the front door and I ran in the darkness. I bolted across the campus, running blind, like a frightened dog. I got to what is known as the PES building when I heard voices, a couple stumbling in the direction of a student village. I hid behind bushes and stayed there, fearful. I eventually made my way home and hid on the balcony unsure what was going on. Later on, a housemate spotted me and he sat with me. For the first time I opened up to him about my family and losing Marcus and Dad. These were conversations I should have had when meeting these people and living with them, but for some reason I convinced myself that this should be kept private. Doing so, made it much more of a struggle until the anxiety completely took hold.

While on my J1 Visa experience in Boston, it became so frequent, happening almost every day. Between socialising, working, the heat, being away from home and house sharing, I couldn't get excited. Instead, I became irritable, scared, panicked and anxious. My only solution was to return home to Ardrahan in Galway.

But being home wasn't the cure to my anxiety. It took some years for me to realise it was an illness that needed to be cured. After some time and reading about grief, I began to recognise my anxious mind and I started to work on it. I wrote every day and began to better understand what was going on. And so I could start helping myself.

It's learning to recognise what triggers the anxiety. It may be events, certain times of the year like anniversaries or holiday season. For me, anniversaries can bring anxiety. Big events with large crowds can also affect me, as can weddings. It's important to learn what the cause is and then you can find something to ease it. When I have a big event coming up, I have a chat with myself and ease my mind about it. As I write this, I have a wedding approaching, one I cannot miss and I am so scared at the thought of it. But I can't avoid such monumental events forever.

These are moments I want to share and enjoy. To deal with anxiety on a day-to-day basis, is chilling out and stepping away from phones and distractions. Sometimes, it's just lying on my bed listening to meditation music and controlling my breathing. Writing is also invaluable as you can track your emotions and see what comes from pen to paper. Anxiety is manageable and it doesn't need to control your life. It may take over at certain times, but remember, you are the boss, and anxiety doesn't own or define you. It's only an obstacle on this journey.

Fear:

As time moves on after a traumatic event, fear can set in. For me, it was the fear of the unknown caused by a tragic death. I became afraid of almost everything. My confidence took a hit, as did my abilities. Fear of horse-riding, fear of driving and just afraid I wasn't 'good enough'. As a youngster I was very brave and had a real 'try anything once' attitude. I was adventurous and always up for a challenge. When I grew older and the fear set in, it really affected me because of how I was as a child.

A few years ago, I was in New York. It was January and very cold. I was away with a partner and our flight home was cancelled due to the snow. He went to the lobby to see about sorting our hotel room for another night. I decided to wait in the room. Once that door shut, I got scared. I panicked and rang him for fear something would happen him between the room and the lobby. I ended up running down after him because the fear was too much in the room.

These were really irrational fears and something that developed in later life for me.

Now I take on my fears one by one. I look at what it is that scares me the most. Once, when I was skiing for the first time, I was at the top of a slope and fear stopped me in my tracks. I could only see the worst along that snowy mountain. I had to talk to myself strongly about it. The next day I was flying down the slopes and enjoying every minute of it.

Another time, a friend and I had booked a once in a lifetime trip to LA and Coachella music festival. She pulled out at the last minute. I couldn't find a replacement so soon and instead of missing out I decided to face my fear and go it alone. A lot of people questioned why on earth I was going to a music festival in the desert on my own but there was so much more to it. This was a challenge that I needed to see through just for myself. And I learned so much on that trip. I was nervous as hell in the tent at night, but I did it and I would do it again.

I am afraid of the dark. Always have been. But I set out to battle my fears, and I made darkness one of those fights. It may be more symbolic than I realised but that was something I wanted to overcome. After LA, I felt like Superwoman.

I live in the countryside, and we have no streetlights just pure darkness between my house and my granny's house. When Marcus was still alive he, too, was afraid of the dark. He would get granny to stand at her door and talk loudly until he reached our house. In recent years, I took on that road. It may only be 100 metres but to me it was like the forest in Harry Potter wherein all sorts of dangerous creatures lived. In reality, there isn't even one tree between my granny's house and mine. Now I walk that road freely, without a care in the world.

I've realised over the years that it doesn't matter how little or how large a fear is, it's taking it on that is important, and overcoming it. I've always wanted to skydive and that is something I need to try and conquer.

Pain:

When I say pain I mean mental and physical pain. The loss of my brother and father was the most painful experience of my life. Mainly the pain in my heart, which at times I could physically feel and thought

I was having a heart attack. I got shortness of breath and ended up going on a heart monitor at the Doctor's. I was shocked and bewildered when the results returned as being perfectly healthy. How could that be? I was in pain. But it wasn't a heart attack, it was heartbreak.

It sounds almost crazy to think that we can manifest mental pain into physical. But supressing emotions such as pain, loss, fear and all I have mentioned can do that to us. Our mind is so powerful. I had to learn to deal with this pain and blockage. Sometimes crying would be enough to heal the hurt. Other times, it was talking to someone professional, or a loved one or a good friend. Every little bit helped me. I used to compete in Community Games when I was younger. I loved running and I was quick. I even represented Galway in the Community Games Finals in Mosney in Meath when I was twelve. I got to travel up for the week in August to compete in the cross-country. I couldn't believe it, I was representing my county and I was bursting with pride. I used to run bare foot but once I qualified for the finals my uncle Peter bought me my first pair of spikes. One thing that has always stuck with me from those days is the motto that the Community Games use – Mens Sana in Corpora Sano, which means Healthy Body Healthy Mind. There at a very young age I was taught the importance of keeping my mind healthy through activity and sport. While writing this book I made exercise a priority. I have been revisiting some very sad times in my life, so I've been going for extra runs outside, following some online exercises and playing tag rugby. It has been so important to me to get fresh air and to move my body.

Happiness:
Finally, something very difficult to deal with at a time of suffering is happiness. Laughing after a loss seems wrong and it can cause feelings of guilt. It is okay to smile again. It is okay to feel happy again and it is certainly more than okay to laugh. Don't ever feel like you cannot feel happiness. It is a fundamental part of life. Laughter they say is the key to life. Can you remember the last time you laughed so hard that your tummy ached? Try to achieve that again. Maybe it's a YouTube video or a film. It could be that one person who has an infectious laugh.

It's important to cherish these happy moments, remember them and feel it throughout your whole body. We all deserve to be happy. Sometimes happiness might be the simplest thing that is right in front of us.

Turning Point

What life says we have to live but one dream?
What life says we must trek down one trail?
Who says we must?
Only us.

A darkened heart and a dampened soul,
A beat-less pulse,
A stiffened smile.

But a deeper meaning,
A stronger quest,
A lust for living.

One body now one soul.
One mind now a dozen dreams.

A grey horizon now shimmering gold.

The sky is bright.
The boreen long.

The shoes are filled.

The blood running strong.

SECTION II

DEALING WITH EVENTS AND SPECIAL OCCASIONS

It'll be lonely this Christmas without you to hold...

The words of Mud, once a classic eighties song but now a devastating reminder during the Christmas season of that empty seat at the table, the lack of gifts under the tree and that one person who you used to spend the day with laughing, bickering, eating and drinking.

For most, the festive season is about family coming together. Extreme happiness and delight on everyone's faces as they tear into presents, eat until they cannot move and lie around the TV watching hours of seasonal movies.

Sadly, when you lose someone you love, that all changes in an instant. For me, this time of year brings with it the exact opposite. And while you can fall into a lonely and despairing trap, there are some ways in which you can honour, respect and share the special day with your loved one.

While decorating a house with lights and tinsel can be extremely painful, it can in some way help. For example, my late brother Marcus, adored Christmas time and he used to decorate the house. After his passing I couldn't bear the sight of a tree and Santa, but then I remembered how much he loved it so we did the opposite and put lights everywhere. Inside and outside, we decorated windows and trees so the house looked like Santa's grotto. Although a sad occasion for my mother and I, the decorations had a way of making us smile because I knew it is what Marcus would have liked. It was also a way of honouring his memory and adding his touch to the winter nights. Every time I see the twinkle from the tree it feels as though Marcus is nodding at me.

We have a crib at home that my parents got when they first married. While the crib is a little worn from playing with it as children and from moving house, we still use it, and it is a little reminder of my Dad who passed as well.

So if you are feeling extra lonely, turn the house into a Winter Wonderland. Get a special star for the top of the tree in memory of your loved one and let it shine bright across your home. Or get a candle in memory of them and light it while you prepare the dinner, have it on the table as you eat and let it cast light into the darkness as you all gather together in the evening. Put your favourite photograph of your loved one into a festive frame and place it on the mantelpiece alongside the stockings. Just because they aren't there in body does not mean they are not there in spirit.

Christmas season brings with it lights, laughter, songs and a lot of festive events. They can be difficult to face up to but it is impossible to avoid it. Walking into any shop you will be greeted with an ocean of decorations and all the classic hits blaring out over the intercom. Before entering take a deep breath and remind yourself what is ahead, and remember, it is just another day.

Invites to parties will be flying in the door and while it can seem too difficult to get dressed up and enjoy a night out, it can offer some comfort. Your loved one wouldn't want you to stop living your life just because they are no longer living theirs. In fact, they would prefer you to get on with your life. It doesn't mean you love them any less or don't think about them. It can bring comfort to catch up with old and new friends. Often in these times when you least expect it, you meet like-minded people at events, even those who have lost loved ones also. They can offer solace and empathise with you.

You may experience guilt for having a good time but that is part of the grieving process. They want to see you smiling and laughing and experiencing life. Don't let the guilt ruin a potentially enjoyable time. Hold a toast for your loved one and let them know you are doing it for them.

The Christmas songs can be the most difficult and harrowing because everyone has their favourite, as did your loved one. My brother's was 'Fairy Tale of New York' and my Dad's, Frank Sinatra songs, so you can imagine how hard they are to avoid. Instead of feeling sad when I hear them I take them as a sign, a 'hello', or a simple gesture letting me know they are with me.

So when you hear that song, remember it is a sign, listen to it, feel the emotion and sing along. And if you are at home turn up the volume and dance around the room. I can tell you it will be a sad day, as will the Christmas after that and maybe after that again, but you have to remember that your loved one wants you to enjoy it as much as possible. Tell stories, leave their seat empty, let them sit with you all, talk to them, talk about them, cry, be sad, be happy, laugh, watch their favourite movie, listen to that song, cry some more. They are by your side, they are listening and want you to enjoy the day.

Birthdays
Another hard time of the year for me is birthdays, be it your own, the one who has passed or someone else in the house.

I loved birthdays and loved celebrating them as a child. I remember having two parties some years because my parents were separated, so I felt like the luckiest girl in the world. Two parties meant extra presents and as a child it was quantity or quality for me. But my 18th and 21st were hard times, I threw two large parties and all my family and close friends came along. We all made the most of the occasion being together in one place, but we struggled, knowing two prominent people were missing – Marcus and Dad.

They loved a good party and were both, in their own right, the star of the show. Dad would always kick off a sing song and Marcus was friendly and outgoing and mingled with everyone. They were the two people you wanted at your party.

But as the saying goes, the show must go on. We had two great nights celebrating my birthday and I even gave a little speech and mentioned Marcus and Dad, not in a very emotional way, but a nod to them.

Equally, their birthdays are a difficult time of year. They both also passed away within weeks of their birthdays. We had just celebrated Marcus' 18th when he was killed, and Dad threw an extravagant 50th birthday before his passing. Both were such memorable nights, marking Marcus' step into manhood and Dad's milestone in life.

One way to help ease the pain during a birthday is to mark it somehow. Don't hide away from it. On Marcus' 21st birthday my family and I got a bottle of champagne, went to his grave and popped it. And standing around his headstone we took a drink in his memory. It was emotional but it also felt comforting and I'll always remember it.

My mother and I also celebrated his 30th birthday, what would have been another milestone.

Marcus' birthday falls on Valentine's Day so, for years after his passing, I would never celebrate the day with my other half. Instead, I would avoid it but that meant missing out on two special occasions in one. Now, I always make the effort to do something that day, buy fresh flowers for the grave, go for dinner and remember him. It is, after all, a day of love.

Anniversaries

With the passing of a loved one comes the annual reminder, an anniversary. Every year around Marcus' and Dad's anniversary I get quite low and a fall into a slump. I've learned over the years to recognise this feeling and I just roll with it instead of trying to hide from it.

For the first ten years since Marcus' passing we held a mass in our local church. As the years went on though, that day would be shared with others from the area that also passed away and I began to feel desensitised from the event. There could be three or four families all sitting in the front to remember their lost one. And it may sound selfish but I felt Marcus should have his own day.

Leading up to the ten-year mark, I asked Mam if she would be okay with that being our last mass. I felt there was no need any more to go to the church for his anniversary. Instead, Mam and I take off somewhere special to remember him or we do something to honour him. While I understand the church is exactly that place for some people, it isn't the way in which we as a family feel we can remember him best.
Saying that, we did spend one anniversary in Glenstal Abbey and went to mass where they honoured and remembered Marcus. It was a special day and the grounds of Glenstal are breath-taking.

Certain days can be a trigger as well as anniversaries. For Mam, she finds Fridays quite difficult, as that was the day that Marcus was involved in the crash. She can get anxious and unsettled. For me, the weeks leading up to an anniversary can be difficult. It is because I am dreading the day itself because it is a stark reminder of whom I have lost and it brings me back to that fateful day.

The most important element when dealing with anniversaries and specific dates is to surround yourself with love. Be it with close family, friends or even animals. Share your feelings as best you can. Write them down, write a letter to your lost loved one, go somewhere that was special to them, and remember it's okay not to be okay.

Weddings
Since Dad has died I have cried at every wedding I have been to, even those where I haven't known the bride and groom very well. As a little girl I always thought I would marry my Dad. When I grew to realise that you can't marry your father, I then focused on my own wedding, as many girls do. The hair, the church, the flowers, all of it.

When Dad died I realised I would never have him to walk me down the aisle or we couldn't have a father daughter dance. So now when I go to a wedding and I see the father walk his daughter down the aisle, I cannot stop the tears. It sounds selfish of me, but I feel so sad that I will never get that experience. The last wedding I was at I caught a glimpse of the bride in her dress as she walked down the aisle and I just focused on her and her dress and tried not to notice her father because I get embarrassed crying in the church.

A father's speech always sets me off crying too. A couple of years ago I was at a wedding. I was invited as a guest's plus one but knew of the families. The father of the bride was a very quiet man but when he stood up that day he gave the most heartfelt and beautiful speech to his daughter and new son in law. I was inconsolable at the table, and remember I wasn't the one who got invited to this wedding.
In recent time I have gotten used to the fact that Dad won't be there to give me away and I have come to terms with it. I have a stepfather and I know he would be just as proud to walk me down the aisle shall it happen.

I say 'shall it happen' because I am not sure yet if I want to have a wedding, certainly not a large Irish one. If I was to marry, it would be somewhere small and it would be a quiet day.

You cannot have a wedding without an engagement. In recent months a number of Marcus' friends have gotten down on one knee. It's such a lovely moment for them and I am so happy to see them all doing so well in life. There is one very close friend of Marcus' who is set to wed. When I initially saw the Facebook post about the engagement I let out a happy gasp. Immediately, I wrote under the photo to congratulate them both. Then I sat back from the laptop and burst out crying. At that very moment it struck me that Marcus was missing out on his friend's special day. I have no doubt he would have been best man.

Then I was sad because that's a moment he will never have, to get engaged and married. I often do wonder what could have been, but then I have to step back and realise that was not his destiny. He will be with us all on special days, on sad and on happy days. When our loved ones die, they only ever leave us in body. And I truly believe that.

Health Is a Crown Worn By Those Who Are Well And Seen Only By The Sick

My Dad died in the Galway Clinic in August, 2006. The weeks leading up to his death were spent inside that place. When it first opened it was often compared to a hotel because it didn't have that typical clinical look to it. It had a grand piano in the main entrance facing a large glass wall that looked onto a garden feature. It made visiting the hospital that little bit easier because, let's face it, nobody likes hospitals.

Dad was in a room that was to the back left of the building. Just as you enter the hall to the rooms there is a quote on the wall. 'Health Is A Crown Worn By Those Who Are Well And Seen Only By The Sick'. I often would read that every time I walked past. But it was a while before the meaning really hit home. When I used to sit with Dad holding his hand, only then did it dawn on me the significance of those words. Here I was a very healthy young girl looking at her Dad fading away and I thought to myself since he had that kidney transplant at 21 years of age he must have been seeing crowns everywhere he went.

We tend to take life for granted. I know I did. I never thought about it much until I lost Marcus and Dad, and why would I? I was a teenager in school. But living all my young life with a sick Dad made me very paranoid. He had been at death's door so often and my greatest fear was that he would die alone. I used to watch him sleeping. If Dad wasn't snoring heavily, his breathing was very shallow.

In 2004, we joined Dad's friends on a holiday to Corfu, a Greek Island. It was my first time on a plane. I was petrified. Dad had these documents that stated he was of ill health and airports always placed us in a lounge. I was a minor at the time and shouldn't have been let in but I was listed as his carer should any health complication rear its ugly head. I remember that nauseous feeling. I was twelve at the time and I was given that responsibility. I was a very tiny child. I looked much younger than my classmates and I was really short. So I looked about nine years old. I was wearing a navy dress with little white flowers on it and a denim jacket. I bought it for the holiday. As I sat on that plane on the runway I felt physically sick. I was afraid first of all of flying and then worried if anything happened Dad, what would we do?

That week I shared a room with Dad. Every night I was either woken by his snoring or by the silence. I would go over to his bed and stare down at him trying to see if he was moving. One night, I'll never forget, he woke up as I was leaning over him and we both got a massive fright. Thinking back now I am laughing. He must have gotten an awful shock and wondered what the hell I was doing. I never told him about my fears over his health and instead kept them all to myself. Marcus used to make fun of me for always sharing rooms with Dad but again, I never told him why I did it. I was always afraid that he would die in his sleep and I never wanted him to be alone. At least if I was in the same room, he would never be on his own.

It was a horrible responsibility but it was one I put on myself. Nobody told me to mind Dad, but I felt he didn't have anyone else. I was his little girl. And looking back now, I am glad I did that for him, because it makes me feel I was able to care for him in my own way.

Over the years I always had a role when it came to Dad and his health. When he moved back to Galway around 2000 we developed a better bond, mainly through horses. I loved them and it became our 'thing'. I got a lovely old horse called Dessie in 2002, and he brought me on leaps and bounds. We did Pony Club together, and we hunted and did cross-country. Every weekend we would be gone in the lorry. Dad and his friend, Tom, started travelling to cross country courses all over Ireland. Sometimes we would be awake at 4 a.m. getting horses ready. We would make flasks of tea and head off. Dad liked it really strong with three sugars and a drop of milk. We all called it 'tar tea'. He never really understood that everyone has different preferences when it comes to tea and only ever made his own type. So on those dark cold mornings as we travelled to the midlands I would drink it to wake myself up. The sugar alone was enough to do that. Dad taught me how to hold a full mug while in a moving vehicle, as he rarely sat into a car without one in hand. Anyone that knew him will remember the Mother Hubbard's mugs that were always lying around his car.

One thing that always came in the lorry with all the gear and horses was his oxygen tank. Dad was told by Doctors to take life easy and to not do anything strenuous like horse riding, but he never listened. We had this great photo of him taken after competing in the Lough Cutra Hunter Trials. He was sitting on his horse, King, on the mobile phone, with a fag stuck in his mouth, and we always said we would send it to his Doctor.

I guess he needed that oxygen tank to keep him going. We would arrive at various courses around Ireland and himself, Tom and I would walk the course together. Some of these courses were two and three miles long, and Dad would get tired. I was always watching him but I was also fascinated hearing him explain what route to take and how to jump certain obstacles on the course. I have to note that I never had a horse of my own at these events, I was brought to help out.

Dad had a bay mare at the time, and Tom had a young grey horse called Harry. I loved Harry. He was sweet and kind whereas the mare was hot and not easy for me to handle. I'd go with Dad and Tom to the start line and usually brought the binoculars to keep an eye on them. A clear round was the aim but I always worried about Dad getting through. As mentioned, his mare wasn't an easy ride.

Just before Dad would set off we would go to the ambulance on site and ask them to be on standby for when Dad would finish. I would make sure that they were aware when he set off on the course. I loved seeing him coming along the home stretch, knowing he was safe. But once he crossed the finish line I would grab the reins, and ambulance personnel would come over. Tom would carry Dad off the horse and he would go into the ambulance. I was always sent back to the lorry with the horses often not knowing how serious Dad's condition was. Dad made sure the horses were the priority here. Getting the tack off them and cooling them down. It was something like a half hour before he would return. I couldn't check on him because the animals were number one. I hated it. But when I would hear him coming back I felt relief. Tom did the driving, as Dad wouldn't be able. For a few days after the competition he was exhausted and needed a couple of days rest, but there was no talking to him. I think he knew his life would be a short one, so he did what he wanted to do. And looking back, I admire him for that, although it came at a cost for the rest of us.

There was another time we were competing at the Dartfield Hunter Trials outside Loughrea. It was April 2005. Marcus was only dead a few weeks. It was our first competition since his passing. Dad and I wore his Garbally rugby shirts and we had black bands on our arms in memory of him. Remember Harry the horse I mentioned above? Dad's friend, Brian, bought him and anytime I needed a horse I borrowed Harry. He was a gentle giant. By now Dad had the black stallion, King Cotton Gold. Together the four of us made a super team. I loved when we competed together, being in the open air working as team. He led me over the tricky jumps and then he let me lead us home. For a very competitive man it felt great that he would let me lead.

On this particular day, he decided to take the stallion out in the Open Pairs. The Open is the more advanced course. I begged him not to go because Dartfield is a long course with a lot of galloping. I knew both he and the horse shouldn't do it. I never once in my life asked Dad to not do something, but this day I made my feelings clear. But he wouldn't listen. He went off and I sat on the back of the ramp, crying. All these competitions are called out over the intercom. So although I wasn't watching I could hear as Dad went around. He was coming to the home stretch and there was a bank to jump onto and off. The stallion stumbled up and came down. I heard as the commentator gasped, 'Maxie Scully is down.' I don't think I ever ran so fast through the fields. My eyes were blurred due to tears. Dad was too far away from me. I heard the commentator say he was on his feet. And what did Dad do? He got back on the horse and finished the course. I was so angry with him. We were meant to compete in the novice competition next. And I refused to do it with him.

But he was a stubborn man and was adamant to go around the course with me. I think for the first time he realised how upset and scared I was. And whether he was able to hide his pain from the fall or not, he convinced me that we could do the competition. We took our time and finished the course, me taking the lead for most of it.

I never understood then why Dad put his body through such tough occasions, but as I mentioned, he must have known his life was going to be cut short. The only problem I had was he never told me. He said he couldn't wait for my twenty first birthday. I was only fifteen at the time and just wanted him around for my eighteenth, so we could head off out together as I was officially an adult. I was sixteen when he died.

Looking back now, I can understand why he led the life he did. I just wish he shared that information with me. Had he told me he didn't have many years then I would have sent him off on horses everyday if it made him happy.

Since his passing I have struggled so much with horse riding. I tried to keep it up for him because we loved it and doing it together was something so strong. The bond we shared while on horseback was something else. One of my fondest memories with Dad was when we took Harry and the stallion for a gallop. They were in Craughwell at the time, on his friend, Jerry's, land. Jerry's fields backed onto the Killeneen turlough. We saddled up and just took off jumping walls until we reached the turlough. Then we opened up. We raced each other through the turlough. Harry was bigger than the stallion and he had a much larger stride. And we won. We bet Maxie Scully. Dad and I had the best fun and greatest laugh over that, and I loved when he would tell all his friends about it.

After his passing, I was out with the Blazers in Craughwell and we ended up going into Jerry's land and taking that very same route. My eyes filled with tears, and although around sixty people on horses surrounded me, I felt sheer loneliness. Another day I remember forgetting that Dad was gone and looking around the field for him. The Blazers wear red coats while the rest of us wear black or navy. Dad always wore a distinctive green coat and it was easy to spot the black stallion too. But both were gone. After Dad died, the stallion was taken away from me. The day he was leaving I went to Craughwell where he was stabled and spent the full day on my own with him. When that horsebox came I was inconsolable and he knew it too. He didn't want to leave. The man that took him told me I could get in contact anytime. A few days later I text to ask how he was settling in, but I never heard from him again.

A few years later, I was in the pub in Ardrahan. We were celebrating because the Gold Cup was around. A man came up to me as he knew Dad, and asked me did I know where the stallion was. I had no clue. But he did and he told me to Google him. That night I got home I did exactly that and there he was, King Cotton Gold, stabled in Edinburgh. I was bawling crying. I emailed the contact straight away to let her know who I was and to see how King Cotton Gold was. She replied and we tried to arrange a visit although it never happened.

In 2010, I turned twenty-one, the birthday Dad wanted to be at. I was a home when my friends called to give me my birthday present. It was a large box. I had to open it all up to reveal what was inside, flights to Edinburgh and a meeting with the stallion. Two weeks later the girls and I headed away to Scotland. It sounds bizarre flying to a country to see a horse, but it meant the world to me. We travelled by train outside of Edinburgh where we were met by his new family. I remember feeling so nervous.

When I turned the corner of the yard and saw that beautiful black head with the snow-white blaze I started crying. And he remembered me too. We had such a special moment. King Cotton was part of my Dad's funeral. When we took Dad out of the church, King Cotton was there waiting. When the coffin came out he started rearing up and pounding the ground. It was the most remarkable sight. I went over to him and he just dropped his head beside me and stood quietly. Back in Edinburgh, I was so happy to see him. He was in a beautiful yard and was treated like a king. They adored him and it warmed my heart. A few years after Dad, King Cotton Gold passed away in his stable. I always feel he returned to Dad.

Nowadays, I prefer to head to my friend Nicola's yard to ride out. There is no pressure and no crowds, just us having fun. I've gone on a few trips with The Blazers and other meets around Ireland but with a surname like Scully it is very hard to avoid the past. It's one of the few places I still feel great sadness, but I also feel closer to Dad when I am out on the horses. They certainly provide a great healing power, as do most animals. Horse riding and the connection to horses is a gift that my Dad gave to me and something I will cherish forever. I hope someday to have my own farm and horses again. Had Dad taken care of himself and stayed away from the horses, both our lives would have been a much emptier place. His ill health made him grab life with both hands and live it to, excuse the pun, the max. He knew how precious life was because he could see all the healthy crowns we wear every day.

Every

With every trying day,
With everything they say,
With every tear you shed,
With every day in bed.
With anger and with fear,
To those far and near,
And then one day,
Everything will be okay.
A Blind Man Showed Me the Light.

A BLIND MAN
SHOWED ME THE LIGHT

(An experience that happened to me
while living in London in 2014)

Taking a walk through Battersea Park I felt out of sorts. With a lot on my mind I almost felt like I wasn't really walking but floating on a cloud. I was feeling a little unsure and apprehensive as I thought about my move back to Ireland, a new job, a new house. It was an experience I should be used to by now, but still never prepared for, and I was beginning to feel somewhat overwhelmed.

We can spend our lives moving and changing yet we are never ready for it. Much like death, we will all experience it at some stage in life, it's inevitable, yet we never know how to deal with our emotions when it arrives!

Back to my walk, I strolled along the path that ran parallel to the Thames. And instead of enjoying the sun beating down on my skin, I was trying to reassure myself with 'how lucky I am, what a good place I am in'. While having this inner lecture, my thought process was interrupted by a scraping noise. It got louder as I walked and I looked up.

What was coming against me was a blind man using his walking aid to guide him along the gravel track. Suddenly, my eyes opened. Here was this man, who could see only darkness, walking alone through a very busy park full of trees, uneven ground and tree roots running in all directions. And yet, he was making his way along seemingly without a bother in the world, probably enjoying the fresh air.

Sometimes we can become engulfed in emotion and see only darkness. We see darkness everywhere we look and at every time of the day, yet we have sight. We have the freedom to walk on any terrain without a walking aid because our eyes guide us over the land we move upon. Have you ever stopped to think how lucky you are to have vision? To be able to stroll in the park, along a street, around your house? The blind man only sees darkness and nothing else. Yet he hasn't stopped living.

He opened my eyes. I ventured further into the park and sat on a bench and watched the world around me. I admired the sun beaming off the trees, which were different shades of green. I watched the water fountain as it danced in the pond. I smiled at all the dogs running freely, fetching a ball, jumping in the pond or lying beside their owners, dogs of all shapes and sizes. How wonderful the gift of sight.

I know many of us experience dark days but watching that blind man made me appreciate the simple things in life, the things we take for granted. We are constantly searching for 'bigger' and 'better', and all too rarely do we take a moment to realise what we have in the here and now.

How blessed are those who have sight, to experience the wonders of the world. We just need to open our eyes and really see the world around us. And, we need to do this more frequently and with more passion. Have you ever stood back and admired your surroundings? Do you ever take notice of the nature around you or close to you? Battersea Park became my haven. It is a large park in London. High-rise buildings surround it, but once I got to the heart of the green area, it almost felt like home. I began to get healing from the trees, and sitting on the grass brought me home to myself, in some way.

I was at a talk recently with entrepreneurs and one man spoke of our thoughts. We can have up to 80 per cent of negative thoughts per day. That is astounding, and it struck a chord with me. Since hearing that statistic I now try and stop myself when I feel I am slipping into a negative frame of mind. One trick I was taught, and it works well for me, is that when it is raining outside, instead of seeing it as a bad thing, switch your thinking to see the positives. The ducks love the rain so think of them. Every time I do this it makes me smile because let's face it ducks are pretty cool creatures. Marcus and I had hens and ducks when we were younger. One duckling damaged its leg so Marcus and I took him inside and we made a miniature splint for him and cared for him indoors until he was strong enough to go back in the hatch with the other poultry.

"DON'T TAKE YOUR ORGANS TO HEAVEN, HEAVEN KNOWS WE NEED THEM HERE."

Maxie Scully died on the 12th of August 2006 after a lifetime battle with illness. He was 52 years of age. While that was very young by today's statistics where males typically die in their 70s and 80s or so, he led an incredible life due to organ donation.

At the age of 19 he got accepted in to the Irish Army Equitation School,

which furthered his career in horse riding. After a series of medical tests, Maxie was struck down with Good Pasture Syndrome. The World Record breaker, and once Irish International show jumper, was told at the age of 21 that his kidney had failed and he was given three days to live. During the Christmas of 1974, his family was told to prepare themselves for the inevitable.

Maxie received a kidney on the 13th of September 1975, which did not take to his body at first. After weeks of dialysis and blood transfusions, Doctors feared the worst. Eventually the kidney made a new home. He went on to live for 30 years and, at the time of his death, was Ireland's longest surviving kidney transplant recipient.

My mother even recalls saying prayers in her school in Gort for him while he was in hospital. I guess kidney transplants were very rare in Ireland at the time, and certainly unheard of in South Galway as far as I am aware.

Upon leaving the hospital, Maxie was told to never drink alcohol, smoke or ride horses, or partake in any physical activities. He later convinced a friend to allow him play on the wing for a rugby game, and with no affects from the game he made two decisions. Firstly, he would never play rugby again, and secondly, he would concentrate on his number one passion - horses.

One evening during the RDS, Maxie watched some amateur horses competing and took particular interest in an 18" chestnut gelding (male horse). Later that night he bargained with the owners and bought the horse named Drumlogan. The next day he signed himself up for the high jump competition. Horse riding is not only a strenuous sport but also takes serious skill and fitness. Maxie defied all the odds that night in the Simmonscourt Indoor Arena in Ballsbridge, he broke the Guinness Book World Record after he jumped the highest jump bareback.

His family and friends said Maxie had reached his goal but that didn't stop the strong-willed man. He went on to have a very successful career in horse riding and wore the green jacket (Ireland) on several occasions. Maxie said how these goals and targets are what got him out of bed every day and drove him to succeed.

With the new kidney he became unstoppable, and so his second love, athletics, became a major part of his life. In the 1970's the World Transplant Games were established. One year the transplant games were held in Japan, and at a press conference, the President of the organization, Dr. Maurice Slapack, was met with criticism by the Japanese who see organ donation as murder of the spirit and it was illegal in Japanese law.

Maurice was puzzled by the questioning when Maxie approached the microphone, where it was said that he spoke so articulately and emotionally of his own experience. The following day a press conference was called which Maxie led. "Transplantation of organs give life, and the spirit of the donor, if anything, lives on," he said. According to the KZN Kidney Association website after a series of questioning by the media, the Japanese Government changed the legislation and legalised organ donation within two months.

In 1995 disaster struck again and Maxie had to receive a triple heart bypass. His then thriving King Conservatory and Double Glazing business had to be abandoned as he began his road to recovery. The horses, though, were never left in the field. Only weeks after having major open-heart surgery, Maxie brought his horse, Kinglogan, to Clonshire to take part in a high jump competition. After training the horse and preparing him, Maxie took a turn earlier that day and decided to hand the reins to his close friend, Michael Blake.

Michael and King broke yet another record but this went unrecorded, or at least it didn't make it into the Guinness Book of World Records.

In the years that followed, Maxie gave numerous lessons and equestrian clinics all over Ireland. In 1997 Maxie organised a charity ride from Craughwell in Co. Galway to Scariff in Co. Clare. The event involved a number of horses to ride through the day and night but only one jockey – Maxie. Followed closely by the Red Cross, he completed the trip in two days and arrived into the East Clare Equestrian Centre on the opening night of the state of the art arena.

His passion for horses and the want to help others was Maxie's ambition, which drove him to his achievements in life. He organised numerous charity rides for the Blazers hunt in Co. Galway and brought along some famous faces to front the ride. Over the years Sharon Shannon, Steve Collins and Irish soccer physiotherapist, Mick Byrne, to name but some, were part of the charity ride.

In the early noughties, Maxie's heart began to weaken and after an assessment in the UK he was placed on the heart organ donation list. Expecting such a major organ one should rest to prepare for the open-heart surgery, but not Maxie. He continued riding horses, took an auctioneering course and opened his own business.

In 2004 he got a new horse, a black cavalier stallion – King Cotton Gold. After weeks of training the new animal he began to compete.

Maxie saw huge potential in the horse and after Ireland's disappointing performance in the 2004 Olympics in Athens, he turned his attention to the 2008 Olympics. He set himself a new goal.

On the 5th of March 2005, Maxie faced his biggest setback in life - he lost his only son, my brother, Marcus, in a car accident. The trauma, pain and shock caused Maxie to deteriorate rapidly. He felt angry that he lived a life of illness and his son's life was cut short. In the months that followed, Maxie's goals slipped further away as his health dwindled. He went into hospital in January of 2006 and he never really left again. He had some minor procedures but they never fully healed. He didn't make it to Marcus' first anniversary mass, which surprised me, as it wouldn't be like him to miss such a special day. That's when I realised that Dad wasn't well. He didn't have the same strength anymore. His energy levels were low. He just wasn't the same man, and the fight in him was fading away. He hadn't that same zest for life. When I was with him I felt I had to be extra cautious should he fall over. On the 12th of August, during his favourite equestrian event, the RDS horse show, Maxie drew his last breath.

He may have only been 52 years old when he died, an age considered extremely young nowadays, but he proved an inspiration. At only 21 years old he was given three days to live, but after a family kindly granted him a new life, a new kidney, he got to live a life of goals, ambitions and fulfillment. He defied all the odds and did more in life than most.

When organ donation week approaches, think about the difference that an organ can make to a life and carry an organ donation card. As Maxie said, "Don't take your organs to heaven, heaven knows we need them here."

Each year, there is a week dedicated to Organ Donation Awareness urging us to carry an organ donation card or opting to donate our organs should tragedy strike. It's something very close to our family's heart and I am forever grateful to the person that gave my Dad a kidney when he was 21, because they added 30 years to his life.

FRIENDSHIPS AND RELATIONSHIPS

One thing that changed for me as I grieved was my friendships and relationships. You see, when grief came knocking on my door at the tender age of fifteen, life, as I knew it changed completely.

My friends were concerned with generally impending exams, texting boys and what outfit to wear to the next disco. All those areas were of interest to me, too, until Marcus died.

Suddenly, I was part of a minority for very few of my friends had dealt with loss. They didn't feel the pain and anguish I felt, nor should they. We were all meant to be young and free. Hurt was meant to be from losing a camogie match or failing an exam, not planning a funeral and burying your big brother. I was screaming with agony on the inside. I needed someone to understand, but equally I didn't want anyone to feel the tearing of my heart.

Returning to school after the funeral of my brother, something had changed within me, a light burned out. Topics of texting and miniskirts no longer appealed to me. Saying that, Marcus used to check to see what I was wearing before I went to discos. One night, I thought I was clever wearing my O'Neill's tracksuit bottoms over my skirt. He was checking on us and I leaned over unaware that my skirt was on show. He gave out to me and made me take the skirt off. That's the kind of brother he was. He used to give me pep talks and warn me not to be foolish around boys and to be aware as some guys only wanted 'one thing'. I admired Marcus for taking on such a father role with me, even though I wanted to wear my skirt going out.

For weeks after Marcus' death, school friends from Seamount stayed over in my house even on school nights. This act of kindness will never disappear from my memory. They didn't understand the extent of my pain but they knew they had to support me. That can be the greatest thing about adolescents, the compassion and care. They too were fond of Marcus and missed him because he always chatted to my friends when they called to the house and, looking back, they probably all fancied him!

After time, I made a conscious effort to be a teenager and I learned to laugh again. As for the opposite sex, it was much more difficult. I remember the day of Marcus' removal I could see some guy friends over the road had stalled, wanting to come to my house but struggling to face the door. This young man's death ran deep with rugby teammates alike, but they came and they sympathised and muttered "sorry" under their breath. These gestures I can still hear. Marcus was very protective of me, and after his passing his friends all took me on as a little sister and watched over me for many years. I always felt protected wherever I went.

In the months that passed I returned to my 'normal' life and that included discos. I'll never forget that first one in Labane Hall in County Galway. I laughed and I ran around the foam that flowed around the dance floor. The girls joined in with me, but the lads were almost afraid and stood back looking at me with sadness, not sure what to say or how to react. I never held that against them - they didn't know what to say.

I moved school soon after, but it was in the same area. I made friends quickly. I could always strike up friendships at ease. But keeping them was my problem.

During the difficult years, when I fell into a depressed state, I pushed people away. Those closest to me at the time felt the brunt of it. I was no longer fun and cheeky, I was a burden, I was depressed, I was lonely. Instead of turning to my friends I made it more difficult for them to be in my company. During my Master's Degree I was in a house share with three other girls. During that time I hit a real low and was put on anti-depressants. I had even worse mood swings. I became erratic. I used to go out all the time because I hated the silence when I stayed in. I needed distraction and sometimes that was the dance floor. But alcohol is a depressant. It made me much worse. I was crying so much during that period in the house. One morning, I was watching Ireland AM, and I was crying into my cereal. Another day I was home for lunch watching Home and Away, all of us were, and I couldn't stop crying. I looked at my housemates confused as to why they didn't find it sad. But they didn't because it wasn't sad, I was.

I was difficult to be around and anyone that was friends with me during that time got pushed away. So I made new friends and moved from group to group. When I met new people I could hide from my troubled past. I didn't need to explain my life, even tell people I had a brother. I could make up my past and present. I thought this was a great idea, until a night out and too much alcohol, I would get upset and tell my story. Then I would panic, and move to a new group. It was a vicious cycle.

I never blame my old friends for anything. They struggled to be around me and I them. I couldn't keep close friendships anymore. And that became part of my relationship pattern.

I was coming out of a long-term relationship when I had that break through. Instead of using that love and connection to take me through the dark times, to hold my hand and help me heal, I too pushed him away. I became selfish with my darkness. I felt lonely and I wanted to be alone. My stubborn nature wanted to let this dark cloud overcome my every being. I wanted to be Beast, locked away from the life I once loved, not wanting Belle to get close to me or even be around me.

I became bitter and angry.

This bitterness took a different course and at that time, reflecting on those months, I thought and let myself believe that my relationships with those around me was to blame. They pushed me away, they abandoned me, they left me like Marcus and Dad did. But I hurt them as well, and it's only over time that I realised what I had done even though it felt like it was too late.

Even upon reflection, I have desperately wanted to reach out to these people and let them know that I'm sorry for the hurt I caused them. But it isn't so easy. We may be connected on Facebook and can see what each other are up to, but that deep understanding has been skewed. I still see some old faces out and about, but it's just not the same. They have changed, as have I.

Sometimes, seeing old comrades brings some pain with it. At times, I felt abandoned and that fragile girl inside likes to remind me of that from time to time. But, I cannot let her take over. I have taken responsibility for my actions.

I was very sensitive and delicate. Like an abandoned dog, I snapped at anyone that tried to connect or offer compassion at that time when I was low. And let's face it, nobody likes a gnarly dog.

Now though, I've come to understand and realise that my grief caused me to do this. My broken heart drove me to the brink. I placed myself in that dark room alone, but I didn't need to go there on my own. I had loving, caring people that were willing to give their time and love to me. They wanted to see me better and they wanted to see me happy, but I couldn't understand that.

In recent times, I have made a connection with some of those people. Be it a coffee, a Facebook message or even a prayer. I only wish the world of happiness for them. I may never rebuild those friendships again, but that's okay too. I've changed, they have changed, we have grown apart. But we will always have those moments and nobody can take those away. We hold special warm memories that far outweigh the pain and hurt. Facebook memories remind us of those college nights even if we don't want to see ourselves eight years ago.

So you see, grief can work in mysterious ways. It's an emotional rollercoaster like no other. It can destroy your life if you let it, but it brings you somewhere new. You have the choice to make a fresh start, to reconnect with those from the past, but to build new bridges also.

I made a new circle of friends and we've built a friendship on honesty and openness. We share happy and sad days, dark and light. We respect each other's past and we try to learn from each other. There have been days that I've been down and I just share a message in our Whatsapp group and my friends remind me how far I've come and how blessed I am. That alone is enough to spurn me on.

As for relationships, I stayed single for a number of years, as I needed to heal and fall in love with myself instead of masking my loss with someone else's heart. Trying to be in a relationship while dealing with grief was very hard for me, I couldn't find the balance. It took me years to pick up the pieces of the grief of losing my brother and father. They had all come together in one massive hurricane tearing through my heart.

Marcus and Dad were the very first men I ever loved, and for years I was afraid to let myself fall in love because I couldn't deal with another loss. The heartache from these losses at one time tore me to pieces and drove me to darkness, isolation and fear. I needed years to heal before I could even dream of bringing another man into my life. The break-up of a relationship can be quite like a death and needs to be grieved as well. You can use the five stages of grief for this. Denial, bargaining, anger, depression and acceptance, they all come to play when a relationship comes to an end.

I got back into dating, but I found a common thread in all. I went on dates wondering, "How long until I scare him away?" It meant that my mind-set became reality time and time again.

A massive aspect of this was my past creeping in. I always wondered when the time would come to mention my dead family members and talk of family is usually first date talk. Something as large as that can make any person uncomfortable. Nobody wants to meet someone for the first time and talk about death. It's not exactly the best scene-setter. At times, I avoided the subject and carried a front for as long as possible but that just made me sad.

I have become stronger in myself, I am independent. I also have a barrier in place, not a wall, just a safe place.

You see, you can't just run and hide from the past because it defines who you are as a person and can shape your future.

I've learned to go easy on myself, to accept who I am, my past and my present. If I am asked about my family, I will speak of them lovingly and honestly, but not with a sad heart.

I've to live my life without Marcus and Dad, and build relationships and friendships my way. They are always by my side supporting me and they will guide me if I need that.

Sharing a life with someone can be daunting and I truly believe I need to be completely and utterly accepting of who I am. I need to care for myself and make my life my priority. I'm learning every day to give and receive love, and not to be overshadowed by my past. I know when I am ready and the time is right I will meet someone perfect, but I am in no rush and not worried.

In summary:
Go easy on yourself, remember that the people around you don't fully understand and that's okay too. If they want to support you, let them, and if they can't then don't hold that against them. After all, we are only human.

As for relationships, be honest with who you are. Don't date someone just for the sake of it. Find someone who loves you, warts and all, who can hold you when you cry, talk to you about your past and who understands that you may be emotional from time to time. Some days you might want to be alone, others you might want to be in a crowded room. We are all different but we all feel the same love, the same pain and the same fear.

DIARY LIFE

As mentioned earlier in my book, I have been keeping a diary as far back as I can remember. I have always loved jotting down my thoughts, and as a youngster it was a place to express myself. Even in school I was constantly doodling on the pages before my eyes. I could not concentrate unless my hands were busy. As I grew I realised how important writing is to me, a place where I could express my thoughts, and understand my feelings. It was a place where I could rant and let loose about certain things I felt I could not discuss openly with people at the time.

I've been reading over some old material from my diaries, entries that are pure raw and from the heart, that capture my true feelings. Some days and even weeks it can feel as though I've returned to a dark place. It may be a trigger such as an anniversary, seeing someone, hearing a song or just getting too busy in life and neglecting myself. Here is one such entry from September 2017.

I've Relapsed Again
It is always a harsh reality accepting that after coming so far to feel back at square one. I've relapsed again. An all too common place at this stage.
When I say relapse I am not talking in an alcohol/drug misuse sense – I am talking about grieving and moving forward with my life.

It has been 13 years since Marcus died and Dad is gone 11 years, and in that time I have grieved and grieved again. I've been to counselling, I've tried every alternative medicine, yoga, meditation, mediums and more. I've studied grief, I've read the books and I've lived with the pain. This time around, it feels as deep and dark as it was back in 2011 when I had my first break through. I was depressed, skipping college, erratic and lonely. I say breakthrough because I don't like the phrase break down.

For months, I have been doing so well. I'd really found my feet. My last stint of therapy was with Pieta House in Tuam, and it was incredible. It was at times extremely tough, heart breaking and difficult, but after weeks of sessions I became strong and focused. And I've been that way for quite some time. But in recent months I have felt myself slip back into my old ways.

I'm confused, lonely, at times desperate and just miserable. I've been trying for so long to shake this emptiness but anger prevails.

This time I am angry at myself for not seeing this coming sooner. I'm hard on myself and I am putting myself down. I am punishing myself and at the same time being punished.

My actions would reflect this. I am hurting myself and doing things that I know are triggers. My mind is playing tricks on me. Leading me into false hope. It's making me question my everything. Trying to suck me down the path of self-destruct.

I'm seeing videos of Hurricane Irma in America and feel that's what's going on in my mind.

It's frustrating because I thought I finally had it all figured out; that I had made my peace with life. That I understood what happened to me and what I want for the future.

Each day, I am learning and growing, some days are just slower than others. Some days I accept what happened, others, I wake up and think it was all a dream.

I have no time limit on my grief. It may take me another ten years, but it is at times like these that I need to be brave. My relapse may be a sign. A time for change, a revival, a re-birth.

I need to sit and try to remain calm as the hurricane passes and then I can reassess the damage, rebuild and reorganise.

It's at times like this that I realise how important it is to look after myself, and by that I mean mentally and physically. We all have a park or area we love to walk along and these places become vitally important at such times.

Throw on some music and wrap up well as you take in some fresh air.

When you are at home light some incense and candles and turn on some meditation music. There are so many beautiful sounds to be found on YouTube – just search 'Meditation Music.'

Get comfortable clothes on, keep warm and try some meditation. Even just listening to the music can help. Try to do some Om's. I know this isn't always easy if you share a house with people, but try not let their presence keep you from doing these things. I usually meditate when I know nobody is around so I can really focus and gain from it.

Write, write and write some more.

If you are feeling yourself getting extremely low, talk to a professional. When I wrote the above diary entry I knew I needed something extra. I had come so far in recent years, I'd visited such dark places that I did not want to return.

Upon advice from a close family friend, I went to see an addiction counsellor. I never saw myself as having an addiction to anything, but there is alcohol addiction in my family and I am always aware of that. I knew that this therapist could better explain addiction to me and the effects it has had on my life since I was a child and how I can overcome my fears and move on with my life.

Those sessions also made me look at my own drinking patterns and made me more aware of the dangers I could pose to myself. Alcohol addictions are so strong in so many families that as individuals we need to take care of ourselves.

Relapse may not be the correct term for me to use, but it felt like I had been cured, and then returned to that dark place. A place that was all too familiar and somewhere I wasn't ready to revisit. But as I mentioned we sometimes cannot stop these things from happening. I took it as a sign to re-evaluate and re-think some decisions in my own life. It was also obvious that I had neglected my self-care in recent months. I got so excited and caught up in all that was around me that I lost sight of my inner self. While life was going so well professionally, I had almost abandoned myself personally.

I've started back at meditation and I am still learning as I go. When I have an evening free I do exactly that, my – self. I turn my phone off and I just concentrate on the things that are important to me. In the chapter, The Importance of Me Day, I have listed some things you can try for yourself.

LETTER WRITING

Over the years I have always written to Marcus and Dad. It is also a method that has been used by various counsellors and healers. I've always found writing to them to be a healing process and it's easier for me to communicate with them when I write. When Marcus died, we, his family and friends, all wrote him messages and notes and we placed them in the coffin with him. It was something very significant to us all knowing that only he knew what each one of us had written. I mentioned that on the night of his crash I stopped into the shop and got Mars Bars for him. Well, I put them in the coffin with him and told him he could have them when he wanted them.

Also, I have very vivid dreams about Marcus and Dad. I always make note of them so to remember them. Some are nice and some are upsetting, but I take them all as signs, and truly feel that when I am dreaming it is them communicating with me. Every dream I have I know that they are no longer here so the emotions within the dream are very real and I've often woken up crying.

In one dream I had, it was my birthday, I was at a horse show and had the same maroon and white horse lorry my Dad had owned. We were all off watching the various classes taking place, it was a warm day as the dust and sand gathered at our feet. I was wearing jodhpurs (riding trousers) and a short sleeved polo shirt.

Dad came over to me and I was so happy and emotional to see him again. He asked me to come back to the lorry with him as he had a birthday present for me. Two puppies sat on the ramp of the lorry. One was brown and white and the other black and tan. They were adorable. I cuddled them and it felt like the best present ever. Then I looked up to smile at Dad and he was walking away. I ran after him, but the crowds were too much as he entered a bright tunnel. I was calling out to him when he told me it was time for him to go back. I wanted so badly to hug him, for him to hold me one more time. I was desperate, trying to grab onto his jacket. I woke up in tears because all I wanted was my Dad.

In every dream I remember about him he is dead, but always delivering some message to me. That dream was so vivid. I often think about the puppies as well because I remember them so clearly and can still feel the joy they brought to me.

Since that dream I have had others, and as mentioned, not all are very nice. After one such startling one, I wrote a letter to Dad because I felt I needed to tell him and explain better what had happened.

January 2015

Dear Dad,

I hope you are keeping well? I'm writing to you because of the nasty dream I had during the week. You gave me a fright. You were so drunk and aggressive, embarrassing yourself and me.

I was very angry towards you and felt it when I woke. I am letting it go bit by bit. Listening to Frank Sinatra makes me realise you did it your way and I admire you for that. If there is one thing I will take from you – it is to do it my way. We all have regrets or lessons learned. I forgive you and I want you to forgive yourself. Let it go – be at peace with yourself. You are in a better place now – you are safe, not suffering, you are at peace, a place of no regrets.

If I can ask you to do one thing it would be to help mum and I. Help me find peace and happiness. Help me to live a life of no regrets, take away my pain and suffering, my anxiety and my fear.

I love you, I always will love you, you are my number one,
Always and Forever, RIP Dad.

As you can see I was very emotional and shaken after that dream. I was almost always asking him for help especially when I was low. To be honest, when I wrote that letter I did feel relief, I felt he was listening and he was trying to guide me on the right track.

Letter writing is extremely emotional and difficult. There have been times I have tried to write but the tears were so heavy that I couldn't see the page before me, or the tears just washed away the words. Here is another letter I wrote to Dad in 2013 when I moved to London.

Dear Dad,
Seven years later and my feet are not on Irish soil but never fear, wherever my heart wanders, your soul is always with me.
For years I wandered and drifted away from reality and lived a distorted 'reality', one where I avoided the pain and loneliness that accompanies death. But last year I stopped running and faced my ultimate fear. I had to let you go. I had to stop holding onto the life I was living, your life. I had to set you free.
Always by my side.

Even reading back over it myself I can see how desperate I was feeling, how lonely and anxious I was. I just wanted some peace in my life, and now I've gotten that. Every day brings something significant, and sometimes we fail to recognise this.

I've written many letters to Marcus over the years too and brought them to counselling sessions where I would read them out loud and then we would burn them, or one time I was told to bury a letter and I did. It is a very powerful way of opening up and letting go. Reading back over the letters above brought me back to those moments and I can feel the heaviness in my heart that I had held onto.

I've even used letter writing for people who are still alive that I cannot speak to. I don't send these letters on. I write them, read them out, and then burn them. And the release this has given me in that moment has been helpful on this journey. As I write the letter, I feel like I am sitting opposite the person and I can hear myself telling them what I feel in my heart. After I finish the letter, I read it out loud and I feel deep down they can hear me.

I plan on keeping up with my writing and journaling my life. Even when I go on holidays I write down the places I visit, even down to the name of restaurants and shops. Being able to write is a gift and I don't mean writing books and thesis. Just scribbling words here and there can offer clarity and peace of mind. Before you move on to the next chapter why not write something down, anything at all that comes to mind. There is no right or wrong here. It's personal and it's your thoughts.

STANDING AT DEATH'S DOOR

Thankfully, I've never been physically ill but I have had struggles with my mental health over the years. But, for me, my struggles were dealing with loss and being unable to cope with loneliness. When I say standing at death's door, I mean that moment you look at it and think, will I do it? Will I walk up and knock on that door?

After losing my brother and father at such a young age it became very difficult to comprehend my surroundings. I had a heart broken mother, grandmother, extended family and friends. Their grief appeared to be greater, but inside I felt I wanted to be dead. When I saw their grief stricken faces at what had happened, I felt at the time, that maybe, just maybe if it was me that was taken and not Marcus they wouldn't be so sad. A very dark mind set.

Those were the feelings running through my mind because everyone around me seemed so miserable and even I felt it too. Marcus was such a strong part of our family and a role model to those around him. We all looked up to him and so many of us depended on him. He was great around the house, he was helpful to the lads at school and he was a shoulder for so many to lean on. I felt I was never as good as him and stupidly thought the world would be a better place to have him back, so maybe we could swap places.

I never wanted to kill myself, but I did think that the world would be better off with Marcus instead of me. He had such a promising future, on his way to securing veterinary college, great at sport and a very popular guy. He had goals, he was driven and he already had a future mapped out before him. He even went as far as having his own house designed, these drawings we still have at home.

Me? Well I just took each day as it came. I probably spent most of my years looking up to him and how studious yet sociable he was. I never thought much about the future, my career or the latter. I was usually content being with my animals, my friends and playing sports.

It was such a dark time and place, and a horrifying thought for a young girl to have. It was also part of the grieving process, as I later realised. After his death, everything I thought I knew about life changed, and changed bitterly. Everyone and everything around me was suddenly incomplete. My life was rocked to the core.

The pain I saw around me made me feel like I suddenly had a purpose and that I was to relieve everyone of their anguish. I thought if I prayed and begged enough, God would take me instead and the world would be a better place.

Dark thoughts for a fifteen year old.

But over time I had to learn that these feelings were all part and parcel of the grieving process. I was going to have to feel and live through every emotion imaginable before I would even begin to understand what was happening to my life.

And I did, overtime. It took time and I had to give myself that.
And I began to realise that Marcus and I had very different paths in life, I had to accept that his was shorter than mine. His life was just eighteen years and eighteen days. He did so much in what was such a short space of time, but that was his purpose. He was studious and he taught me how to prepare for exams. Not long before his death he and I were both studying for the Leaving and Junior certificates. At the weekends, he would be in his room, head in the books and I would be watching TV. He would come to the living room, turn off the telly and he would do a deal with me. We would both study for a while, then take a break together. And that is what we began to do. Study for an

hour or so then watch TV, have tea or go outside playing rugby. Three months after he was gone, I had to sit my Junior Cert. And each day I did exactly as he taught me: study, break, study, break. He also trained me how to throw a rugby ball correctly because all those times we spent in the garden weren't just for fun, it was so he could practice. I now play tag rugby so those mini training sessions in our garden in Ardrahan were beneficial. You see, his life was cut short but he made sure to set me up for mine. That is the type of selfless person he was.

For me, there was so much to do and achieve. My goals and ambitions came and I realised what I wanted from my life. I had to deal with the losses I was dealt and had to learn from them. Then, when I began to see the light and return from a place of darkness, I created and followed my dreams, plans and hopes.

Much of my recovery came from reading material about grief, talking to professional people as well as those who had experienced loss. My writing also became a massive part of learning and growing. Even now I still pick up old diaries and to see the changes, and the difference in the years amazes me. In 2012, I struggled to get out of bed and attend my lectures for my Master's Degree. I managed to get a first class honours, although at times I was sitting at the desk but I was never present in my mind. I could see only dark clouds and the negativity around me. I did not think I would be able to pick myself up. But I did, and went on to do things I never expected. I landed an internship with MTV in London, and while not ready to leave the nest, it was probably the break and space I needed to learn and grow. At times I was incredibly lonely in London, but I did so much soul searching as well as actual working that it took me to the place I am today, career and health wise.

London can be the most amazing city, but is also incredibly lonely. I found people plan weekends in advance and a lot get out of the city then to the countryside. I rarely ventured beyond the zones of the tube line. I was in London for a brief stint, and always knew it wouldn't be long term. The weekends were extremely long. I am not great at relaxing and watching hours of TV. I prefer to be out and about. My housemates weren't around much and usually funds were low due to the cost of living. At first I struggled to fill my weekends and found I was getting down. Though, I soon learned to make a life for myself. On Saturdays I would get up and get out. I walked to other areas of London and went for coffee in different places, my pen and paper in tow. London is where I had to put myself first, simply because I was alone on the weekends and had no other choice. I learned to enjoy my own company, to sit in a café on my own and to read in the park. If I relied on other people I would never have discovered what I really wanted in my own life, and I also had to learn to deal with my feelings of loss and loneliness.

The process of grief has taught me so much over the years – to be patient, caring and kind to yourself. I know it seems easier said than done, but once you learn and understand that grief has a process to it, you can begin your own recovery and journey to acceptance.

Often these days people throw words like mental health, suicide, and anxiety around, but some don't really explore their inner feelings and that can be detrimental. We read and see so many comments on social media but how many of us actually do anything about it? While reading a nice positive message can make us smile, we need to go that extra mile. Use it as a sign to get away from the superficial world of social media. Go write, read or meet a friend face to face. Talk to people in the real world. Call an old friend, research various ways of healing, which I have spoken about in this book (chapter on Alternative Healing).

Looking back now and reliving those thoughts about wanting to swap places with Marcus absolutely frighten me to realise I was that desperate and consumed by what had happened. I've learned to love myself and the life that I have been given. Sure, I have been dealt an unfair hand but now I must learn to live with it and learn from it. I remember when my mother first heard about these thoughts and she was so sad, even looking at her face I realised those thoughts were wrong but I also knew they were just that – thoughts. I know too that Marcus is with me every step of the way, he is experiencing life through me. He is enjoying seeing me make and achieve my goals in life. I know he, along with Dad, is very proud of me. And I enjoy knowing they are with me on this journey. Sure, I have made a few mistakes along the way but that is all part of living and learning.

It is a long road and something that has to be treaded carefully. Being brave isn't about announcing your problems to the world. It is about taking the first step down the road less travelled, accepting that you want to move on with your life, that you want to heal and learn to love again. That even in the darkest days, hope will prevail.

There is no greater feeling than waking up feeling refreshed and energised, you've had what feels like the greatest sleep and you feel you can take on the world. Maybe you've a nice day planned with family and friends or you are ready for the working day and to give 110%. You're smiling through the day and giving a nod to those you pass along the way. The sun feels like it's shining right down on you. You feel today you can achieve everything and more.

Then it hits you.

The guilt of feeling okay. You woke up smiling and now you feel the dark clouds come over you. That is living with grief. Here's a diary entry I wrote from a time when I felt my life was going so well and then that guilt hit me.

The past couple of months seem to have whirled by before my hazel eyes. And maybe that is because I've been on an even keel for some time now. I turned a leaf late last year or I should say I began to turn a corner. And from then on I built on it and it grew, and for the first time in years I felt I had grown the wings that had been clipped when I was fifteen years old.

But then life was going so well that it almost scared me. I know it sounds bizarre, carrying a weight for a decade only to feel somewhat frightened and unsure when it lifts.

You see, I became accustomed to the life of grief that I forgot what it was like to live with happiness every day. When great things started happening to me I found it difficult to understand why I was having such a run of luck and at times held myself back in case it was only temporary. But almost a year on I've learned to juggle the really great things in my life because, at the end of the day, grief is with me, it is in me and it has defined an entire decade of my life, so it will always be by my side.

And how do I know this?

One year, during World Day of Remembrance for Road Traffic Victims, and while I couldn't partake in any events taking place, I did share a photograph marking the sad occasion. And while everything was going swimmingly that weekend, the day hit me like a tonne of bricks, much more than I expected.

Sharing that photo brought it all to life again, while Marcus is my brother, he is in fact a statistic, a number that is sadly increasing. To me he is my family but to others he is a number in a long line.

But what struck me the most was how low I became. In the days that followed I wasn't myself and I slipped back into my old self. Something that frightened me. Because after all the work I had done over the past twelve months, I thought it was short lived.

But I overcame it, and realised I have to be easy on myself. While I'm much happier now, I have to remember that it is okay to have some down time. That feeling lonely isn't necessarily a bad thing. It is a part of my life and makes me appreciate the better times.

As Oscar Wilde once wrote:

"We are all in the gutter but some of us are looking at the stars."

ATTACK THAT PANIC ATTACK

I think it's fair to say that we all fall victim to panic attacks and anxiety at some stage in our lives, some more often than others. For me, my first panic attack I can remember came when I was very young. It was in the RDS Horse Show and I was roughly 11 or 12 years old. My Dad and I went every year and we parked the horse lorry in Ballsbridge, Dublin for the entire week. Dad always let me do as I wanted once I checked in every hour or so, which I always did. I made so many friends during that time. Dad's lorry was also a focal point at the show. Everyone would gather and hang out at it.

Dad knew the lads in charge so we got extra space around the lorry, and we were the only ones allowed to connect to the mains of the Simmonscourt, meaning we had electricity at all times. Thinking back, most people would charge their phones with us. Dad always had an abundance of sweets as well. It was a very special place and I've some very fond memories.

One night I was invited to stay in the lorry next door with a friend. They had a brand new state of the art one that was finished to the highest quality. It was like I got a free upgrade for the night. As the night drew on and we went to bed, I could not sleep. I felt anxious and upset for no apparent reason. Around 2 a.m. and with no hesitation, I got up and went back to my own lorry. That was my first memory with anxiety and panic attacks.

From then, the next time I can recall getting them was while on my J1 student visa trip to Boston in 2011. It is meant to be the most carefree time of any student's life, living the American Dream. House sharing, working odd jobs and partying. For me, it was all too much. I started having panic attacks. I remember sitting in the living room in our cramped, hot apartment, clutching onto the windowsill, feeling this dread and fear consume me. I couldn't breathe. I just wanted to open my eyes and be at home back in Ardrahan in Ireland.

These panic attacks and feelings of profound anxiety became a daily thing, and I knew I just had to go home. So I cut my J1 short as I knew in my heart that I had to be close to home and try to stop these. I often reflect on some of those occasions and at that time, I thought I had a heart condition, in fact I was convinced of it. It was only when I realised I was grieving that I was able to start to make sense of those feelings.

When I was living in London and working for MTV, I kept everything about my past quiet. Only if people asked me directly did I tell them about the deaths of my brother and father. I threw myself into work and had a very busy social life. Whenever I felt anxious or upset at work I used to go to the toilets, hide and cry.

To give some background to working with MTV, it all started after I finished off a TV training course in Dublin with The Park Studio. They sent out emails about jobs and I saw MTV were looking for interns. Never in my wildest dreams did I expect to get noticed for it. I was a girl from Galway who dreamed of working in Dublin, not London. I applied anyway, because at the time I was unemployed and my mother wanted me to be actively looking for work. I applied for every single job in Dublin within the field of media, everything from unpaid work to actual roles. I never got a reply from even one place, which left me disheartened. I had a degree in media, a Master's in Journalism and experience in the field. To anyone who is struggling to find work, never give up, follow your dream. What's for you won't pass you.

One year after my brother's anniversary mass, I was chatting to his friend telling him I was struggling to find work and he said to me, "When it rains it pours," and those words stuck with me. It's like waiting for a bus, you may be ages standing around and then suddenly three or four come together and that is what job hunting can be like.

Back to MTV. I had just moved to Dublin in late February 2013. The first week of March I was coming home for Marcus' anniversary mass. I was getting the bus from Dublin city and it was the 5th of March, Marcus' actual anniversary date. I saw an email and ignored it but as I sat on that seat and the bus pulled away, something inside me was urging me to read it. It was from a lady in Viacom telling me I had been shortlisted for a role with MTV and could I fly over the following Tuesday. This was Friday evening. I rang my mother in shock. Something significant has always happened to me around Marcus' anniversary.

That weekend I booked my flight and hotel in Camden Town. On Monday I flew over and was quite nervous as I didn't know London all that well. My friend and neighbour from Ardrahan, Chloe, was already living in London and she met me that evening, took me for my first ever Nando's. It wasn't in Ireland at this stage so I felt very privileged.

The next morning I went for breakfast and made my way to Hawley Crescent where MTV is located. It was mesmerising. Once I walked inside I knew straight away that this place was meant for me. I met another Irish girl whom I was in Miss Ireland with in 2009. She too was here for the role of MTV News Intern. How exciting two Irish girls from the country made it to the top five out of hundreds of applicants.

We spent most of the day in the building doing some group work, a quiz and then one-on-one meetings with our potential bosses. In that interview I got on great and felt confident about the task. I left MTV that evening and made my way to the airport as I only came in for that night. I was going through airport security and in London it takes a little more time than Irish airports. As I made my way through the airport I checked my phone and I had a missed call. Without hesitation I called the UK number back and then I was told, "You have the job, you're starting in two weeks." I screamed with joy in Heathrow that day.

After four weeks of having an apartment in Dublin I had to move back out and pack for the UK. I had nowhere to stay when I first moved over but found a place to lodge with a lady also called Scully. It was like home away from home. I started in MTV, and within weeks I had a brand new apartment in Brixton. I even started dating someone so my life just seemed perfect.

But in a few short weeks the bubble burst. I let everything get on top of me. I tried to cover the cracks but that feeling of being away from home set in. Some of which I brought on myself as I convinced myself it was all too good to be true, and that I didn't deserve such happiness. That can be a very dangerous mind-set. I was almost wishing my good fortune away as soon as I got it. It took me some years to work on that area and allow myself to accept good things can happen and I do deserve the very best. We all do.

I worked really hard in London. People in the office used to comment that they always saw me running everywhere and it was true. Running errands and running from my feelings. I was up and down the stairs and all around the building all day long. I was the 'yes girl'. Being an intern I was afraid to say no to anyone. I did every job that every person asked of me. I was one of the first on my team to be in work and always the last to leave. Some days I put in twelve-hour shifts but there was no overtime paid. I convinced myself that if I worked very hard that my reward would come. I built up my CV to the best I could. I was trained in lighting and sound. I operated TV cameras, managed the studio, did research, managed the video content on the website, interviewed people, went to red carpet events, and anything else that was asked of me. I never once complained, just cried in the toilets. Looking back I shouldn't have spread myself out so thinly and should have looked after myself more, but I wasn't ready to put myself first.

The truth is, I was burning the candle at both ends. London life is very fast paced and I got a little over excited. There were parties galore, every night of the week if I wanted and they all had free bars. This seemed like the best life ever. Late nights and long days took their toll. When I walked in those doors of MTV my dream was to be a TV presenter, when I left I wasn't even sure I wanted to work in the media, because every sparkle inside me was diminished. The exhaustion and mounting grief was too much to take.

In October of 2013, we all went to a massive Halloween party. Everyone from MTV past and present went along. It was a celeb filled event and I was so excited to be asked. Halloween is the party everyone wants to get invited to. We all got ready together in the office and made our way to the venue. I'll never forget a colleague gave out to me as a teacher would for spilling fake blood on the floor. She made me feel like I was some little stupid girl. As the night wore on, I was feeling trapped. Everyone was unrecognisable in costume. There were people dressed as unicorns and so many dressed as dark Halloween creatures. I remember feeling frightened and overwhelmed by it all. I got a massive panic attack and had to be taken to a room upstairs.

I'll never forget my boss sitting down with me and talking about it. He told me that I should have been more open with everyone in the office, they cared for me and didn't want to see me like this. I didn't have a panic attack again for years due to his kind words because I suddenly realised I wasn't alone and I did not need to keep it all inside.

Upon reflection, my panic attacks in later years were a result of the unresolved grief. I bottled up the pain and suffering for so long that it had to rear its ugly head in some shape or form. People around me needed to know what was going on. So now I look back and realise that maybe they were all signs. Signs that I needed help, needed to talk to someone and needed to address my true feelings and emotions.

I've suffered with panic attacks in the past and still get them, but very rarely these days. I now know when they are coming and, over the years, I have picked up some tips and tricks that help ease them, soothe that helpless feeling and learn to recover, which I have listed below for you.

As I have said before, I am not a Doctor nor am I a psychiatrist, I am just a girl who got fed up with getting anxious and not having control and I decided to face it head on and tackle it.

Here are some tips and tricks that help me:

1. Rescue Remedy: I find the little bottle my saviour. I keep it beside my bed and on my desk. Some mornings I wake up, maybe after a nasty

dream and that dread sets in so I take some drops under my tongue and before I know it I'm off out the door enjoying my day, provided I am not driving as some rescue remedy contains alcohol so always read the label. Use it flying as well and anytime I feel any sense of panic come over me. And sometimes before bed if I am restless I take it then also.

2. Water: Our bodies are made up of so much water and drinking a glass when you feel panicked eases the mind. Sometimes we can get so caught up in life that we forget to breathe and take a step back. A glass of water, while hydrating you can bring you back to the present moment. It also helps with headaches.

3. Fresh Air: The oldest trick in the book. A brisk walk outside can relieve a panic attack, even just a walk around your garden. When I was working in Dublin and London I used to get out and walk around the building or block. The fresh air and brisk movement helps to relax and allows time to gather those thoughts that are running so wildly around your head. Even while writing this book I got out as much as possible to get fresh air and to take a break.

4. Tea: Sure, doesn't tea fix everything. And although I love my Barry's Tea, herbal teas can be great to help relax your body and mind. Lately, I've taken to drinking caffeine free tea after a certain time of the day and I cannot recommend chamomile tea enough. I take a bedtime tea every night before bed and I feel all warm and mushy going to sleep. Be careful of over consumption of caffeine, especially coffee. Anxious people should be very wary of it.

5. Writing: I've always been a huge fan of keeping a diary. Writing is such a good source and it can help so much when you get to see your thoughts on paper. It offers release and also helps to understand what is happening once you see the words before your eyes. When you are feelings anxious or panicked try scribble down some lines of what you are feeling and what is the root to the emotion. And always finish with the things you are grateful for (family, friends, pets, etc.).

6. Breathing: Something we do all the time yet take for granted. When you feel a panic attack coming on your breath sharpens and suddenly catching it becomes a task. If you sit on the floor or in a hard chair, close your eyes and take deep breaths, in the nose and out the mouth. When you exhale picture yourself letting every worry and stress go. Stay doing this until you feel relaxed. Relax into the chair or the floor below you, drop your shoulders, relax your limbs and breathe. Stay for as long as you need, until you feel that panic lift. I usually throw a meditation playlist from YouTube and lie on my bed or yoga mat for this. I lie on top of the sheets and across the bed so I know I am not going for a nap.

7. Music: This may or may not help but I am a massive music fan and I have certain songs that trigger an emotion. 'My Way' by Frank Sinatra was played when my Dad died and Robbie Williams 'Angels' was the song played at Marcus' funeral. Whatever music makes you smile or helps you relax, play it and sometimes it can take you away from the panicked moment or help that sheer anxiety pass. I listen to meditation music all the time while I am doing jobs around the house. It makes me feel mellow. Sometimes though I need a good dance to shake things up so I will throw on something louder and lively.

8. Touch: You know that sensation when your mind begins to run away with you and you are living in the past or the future but not in the now? That happens to me far too often and I forget the present moment. It usually occurs when I am in bed and instead of shutting off, Mario and Luigi decide to run laps around my head. I was introduced to the sense of touch some time back. I place my hands on my pillow and the bed sheets and remind myself where I am – my bed. It is something so simple and effective to bring my mind back. And soon my mind registers that I am in fact going to sleep. I use this technique throughout the day and find it very effective.

9. Lie Down: If you feel rather anxious and uncomfortable try to lie down for a few minutes. Lie on the floor and just breathe. Close your eyes and let your body rest on the floor. Open your hands and imagine the air around you gently surrounding your body like a protective sheet.

Let it wrap lightly around your entire body and almost feel the softness and security of it holding your every limb while you unwind.

10. Talk: No matter what we all have that one person we can talk to. Even if it is only on Whatsapp or Facebook, it's having someone to share the feeling with, reason things out and assure you that everything is okay. And if you really feel deep down that there is nobody you can talk to, then tell your dog or cat or even the bird outside the window. After Marcus and Dad passed away I found horses a great comfort to me. I could talk to them and they had a way of knowing I was down and would stand still with me. I also have my dog and cat, Bella and Baba, and I find them very soothing. The connection between a pet and an owner is unbreakable. My dog keeps me active and makes me go outdoors whereas my cat will come in when evening falls and just sit with me on the sofa.

I hope these tips and tricks can help you. Once you realise that so many people have experience with panic attacks, it can lift a burden and the pain, and ease them. Those kind words from my boss that day were enough to help me in that moment. He didn't give me any specific advice nor did he offer a cure, it was just that reassurance that I didn't have to be ashamed or hide away.

But always remember that professional help is available. Never be reluctant or embarrassed about it. People have trained to help you and it is the best investment you will ever make.

A ME DAY

TAKING TIME OFF

It's so very important to take time out from the concrete jungle, the busy work office and re-evaluate and reflect. We can become so caught up and consumed by the everyday noise of life around us. Checking our phones, looking at apps, updating our social media channels, checking them again and again. How many times have you looked at your phone already today aimlessly without actually doing anything useful on it? Just browsing and swiping, looking but not observing. I read an article in The Irish Examiner that used the term Screenager to describe young adults and phone usage. According to statistics, teenagers are spending roughly nine hours a day looking into a phone screen. It is alarming but I am not surprised as I am guilty of excessive phone use and looking at my various social media accounts.

Then we become obsessed with other's lives. I, too, am a culprit of this. Seeing someone I don't even know posting a carefully calculated photo by a beach that's Photo-shopped and wishing that was me sipping on that fresh coconut. Seeing cute photos of men proposing to girlfriends or the lavish gifts they have given them - losing sight of the fact that these photos are only created for Instagram and for us to hit *like*, and grow this person's online persona when, in actual fact, it's false. Always online, always active, updating all social media accounts, staying in the know for fear of falling behind. I watched an episode of Black Mirror called Nosedive that looks at social media ruling our everyday lives. In the episode, people are given points and an average score on their social media use and activity. People rate each other and if you receive a low score it brings down your average. Having a high rating means you can avail of certain perks like living in nicer housing estates, renting better cars. Have a low rate and you cannot avail of the finer things in life. It is a stark reminder that our society could be headed that way. In that episode people were living false lives to attain high scores to live what seemed like the picture perfect lifestyle.

Social media jealousy is nasty and can give us a sense of insecurity about so many aspects of life. It is so vital to step away from this world, detach and look after number one – yourself. Take a 'Me Day'.

One day recently I woke up, turned my phone off and took a Me Day. I gave myself time to reflect on recent happenings, my current situation and what I want in the future. It is so easy to get distracted and caught up in the bubble especially when you work in the 24/7 digital era.

Fear is one of the most tackling of emotions. Fear of missing out. Fear of not being up to date with the digital age. For me, fear holds me back in everyday things. It rears its ugly head every now and then or when I try push the boundaries or test myself. Sometimes, I put myself out there but the fear takes over and I retract. But enough is enough, how will I ever succeed if I let this take control? That's when Me Day stepped in.

So for my *Me Day* here is what I did:
1. *Woke Up and turned my phone off*
2. *Meditated*
3. *Made a hearty breakfast*
4. *Did a workout (1 hour at home workout from YouTube or any form of exercise that works for you)*
5. *Wrote in my diary*
6. *Had tea with my neighbours*
7. *Tidied up my room*
8. *Had a good chat with my Mammy*
9. *Did some personal admin (important emails and a to-do list)*
10. *Relaxed with some incense burning*

I know for so many people it seems impossible to take a day off but would it really be the end of the world to take even a half day? To spend some time on yourself? To get away from the pocket sized emotional controller?

When I lived in London, it seemed impossible to take time out. But I remember I booked one Monday off and spent the entire day doing things for myself and it was the refreshing break I needed.

It's also something very difficult to do. Spending time on myself? Are you mad? After I meditated, I had a cry for myself. But I felt a release after doing so. And then I realised I was upset over something out of my control.

I had some niggling issues going on in my personal life and even talking about them to family and friends helped me to see everything more clearly. I even caught up with an old friend who reassured me of some future plans I had.

As nighttime approached I had clarity and a greater understanding of what I am doing and I'd made some plans for the future.

So make the decision to have a 'Me Day' and reap the benefits.

THE FIVE STAGES OF GRIEF

(From the book - Mental Health for Millennials)

Death doesn't destroy us, it defines us. Living with grief is the most obscure, misunderstood and painful experience for those of us living and breathing. We will all die one day. Nothing or no one can ever prepare us for the hurt, the suffering, the loneliness and destruction that death can leave behind. But we are all in this together and we all have each other.

The Taj Mahal in India is described as one of the medieval Seven Wonders of the World. It is a mausoleum that holds the remains of the wife of the famous Moghul Emperor, Shah Jahan. Reports from that ancient time say that he could have had any woman in all of the land but he, instead, chose Mumtaz Mahal, a beautiful and intelligent woman who was a devout Muslim and a great helper to the poor. She died in 1631 after giving birth to their fourteenth child.

The distraught Emperor began to build the mausoleum immediately for his wife. Thousands of skilled labourers worked on the marble domed building and no expense was spared. The Indian poet, Tagore, described the architecture as 'a tear on the face of eternity'. The distraught Emperor never re- married and 35 years later he was imprisoned in a fort by his son where he could see the Taj Mahal and following his death he was buried beside his wife.

Ancient history gives us some of the earliest accounts of the grief suffered by different cultures and worlds.

King David expressed his sorrow in a lament that is included in the Old Testament, and Achilles vowed he would not bury Patroclus until justice had been served.

These stories remind us that we all experience grief in different forms yet we all feel the same pain and suffering, the loneliness and the anxiety.

My Personal Story

On the 5th of March 2005, my heart was ripped from my little body and shattered into millions of tiny pieces. At fifteen years of age I tried desperately to retrieve all those little pieces and mend them back together again. My big brother, Marcus, was taken away from us in one foul swoop. He was eighteen years and eighteen days old. A young handsome, strong and clever man with more than the world before him, he was everybody's friend and nobody's foe. Lads wanted to be him and ladies wanted to be with him. That fateful night, he returned to rugby training after being absent due to an ankle injury. His friend, Cathal, had his own car and the pair headed off, almost on an adventure, but one we didn't realise it was to be their final one.

At nine o'clock in the evening, whether it was driver error or inexperience, there was a crash. Our dear neighbour, Cathal, died on impact but Marcus was alert and speaking. He apparently talked to the paramedics and just wanted to get away from the wreckage. We heard that he attempted to answer his ringing phone that he walked from the car to the ambulance all signs to me that he was doing good, maybe a little sore.

But something changed once he stepped into that ambulance – it's almost as though he didn't want the now large gathered crowd to see him hurt – he wanted those eyes to see the Marcus they all knew.

As the hours rolled by, Marcus' condition deteriorated. My mother, Pauline, asked that we see him before he went for surgery. At fifteen I was still completely oblivious to the fact that my brother was in a serious state. I'd brought his favourite chocolate, Mars bars, with me to have ready for when we could see him. That's how my mind was working.

The nurse led us to the resuscitation room and the sight of that worried me. After years of watching ER, I knew this wasn't a good place. In my shocked state, I understood that Marcus was walking and talking after his accident and thus was puzzled as to why he needed to be in the resuscitation room.

I'll never forget what I saw before me. Marcus was unconscious on a bed. Pipes and machines everywhere. That monitor I used to see on my TV screen every Sunday night was now before my naked eye. Why wasn't he awake and talking? Mam and Dad scampered to his head and the Doctor's words hit me, "Be careful not to stand on those tubes, they are his lifeline."

Why was I suddenly living my own episode? And to explain my innocence, I was waiting for him to wake up because on that show, they save everyone. But this wasn't some TV studio, there was no camera rolling, this was real life and in real life, things aren't always rose tinted. Marcus tilted his head and suddenly he was awake or so I thought. The nursing and medical team were empathetic towards us. **Just reality. No false hope. S**o many questions running through my head. I was surrounded by people. But totally alone. Devastated.

"That's the tube moving his head," I was told.

Why was he asleep and why did he have all these tubes and why was the room in complete chaos? The next few hours were long yet I saw many acts of kindness that night in the waiting room. A rather eccentric lady was rummaging about. No business in the place from what we could tell, perhaps sheltering from the cold of that March night or in to chat to such forlorn faces. She got some potato chips from the vending machine and although the room packed full of friends, neighbours and complete strangers, this lady was offering out her snack to us all. A welcome distraction. Maybe she was an earth angel sent there to distract us from the impending trauma.

By 2.30 a.m. Marcus had given up his fight. I don't know if he ever really was alive once the cars collided. I often think he just spared us those few hours, almost saying goodbye in his own way.

The days and the months that followed were harrowing. At the age of fifteen my only worry in the world should have been what cover to put on my phone. But at home life was traumatic. My parents were torn to pieces. I could see the fragments break away each day from their souls.

My father, Maxie, lost more than just his soul. His heart was broken beyond repair. I felt like the most helpless and useless being at that time. When they cried, I wanted to take the hurt away but I couldn't possibly hold any more. My own was weighing so heavily on me, but I felt I had nowhere to share it, even expose the hurt and the trauma. I thought if I just hide it away, it would disappear. It's like something or someone was determined to break me.

In August 2006, my Dad lost his own battle with illness. I watched him fade away before my very eyes. Again, helpless. I was screaming inside for him to fight another day, not to give up. He had been battling illness for most of his life, surely he could battle some more. I wasn't ready to let him go and I sure as hell wasn't letting him leave me like Marcus did.

But by sixteen, I had no answers or power to save him. His frail body was exhausted, his heart weak. At least I got to hold his hand as he slipped away and now Marcus wouldn't be alone. It was just Mam and I.

Home was not an easy place. The walls were stained with anger, sadness, fear and depression. School was my haven. It was fun and a place where I could be silly and light hearted. I couldn't stand the idea of any form of drama so I spent much of my time playing sports such as camogie and Gaelic football. On the field, I wasn't the girl who lost her brother and father. I was a player and I had a role to play on my team.

When my brother and I first came to Ardrahan from Spiddal we hadn't played much GAA. In fact, I never had. We both joined the respective hurling and camogie teams. We didn't come from a strong GAA background so we both fought hard to make our place on that starting fifteen. To me midfield was where the best players played and that's what I worked towards. When Marcus passed away he had earned that prized position. And following his death, so did I. Reflecting now upon those years, perhaps the field was escapism for me.

As the years went by, I shut myself off emotionally. I steered clear of upset and anger but inside told a different story. I was frustrated at keeping up the act, at always having a smile across my face. Years of pain, anger, fear and torment raged inside me like a wild beast.

It was rare that this specimen broke free but when it did, all hell broke loose. When I went to University and started drinking that's when I couldn't control it. On a night out and after lots of alcohol your inhibitions are different and often times if someone made a passing comment about my outfit, I would get so upset and angry. At the time, I genuinely thought the emotions were aimed at this person, but in reality, it was the bottled grief. And in the early hours of the morning we would make our way home, exhausted and weary it would crawl back into the dark hole never to be spoken of.

During 2011, breaking point hit. I called it a *breakdown* but my mother called it a *break through* and reflecting on that time, it was exactly that. I felt as though my world was crashing down around me but, in actual fact, it was an awakening. I was given the space, the time and the energy to feel the love and the pain, the laughter and the tears, the darkness and the light. It was a time of discovery and of healing. And it is where I began to understand the complexity of grief and the many different stages within its process.

I learned that there are five stages, denial, anger, bargaining, depression and acceptance and that these are a part of the framework that makes up our learning to live with the one we lost. They are tools to help us frame and identify what we may be feeling. I also learned that not everyone will experience all of them or in a prescribed order.

The Five Stages of Grief

Elizabeth Kubler-Ross, author of *On Grief and Grieving* provides a detailed description of the 5 stages of grief.

The first stage is denial. This is when you know that your loved one has died but when you are sitting at home, you cannot believe they are dead and you are almost expecting them to walk in the door or call. You may be in a dream state whereby you are waiting to wake up to find it was all just a nightmare.

This state of denial allows the grieving person a mere moment where the pain of loss doesn't exist.

Denial is a way of survival, which may be hard to comprehend when you feel your whole world has been destroyed. When we are experiencing denial, the world around us becomes meaningless. Things that once seemed so important and overwhelmed us are pointless and irrelevant. *"Denial helps us to pace our feelings of grief."*

For me, denial was almost immediate. When we were in the hospital and the Doctor came to give us the devastating news, I didn't believe him. Even as my mother and father clutched me close to them, I wanted to push them both away because this was not happening. How can an eighteen-year-old man be dead? How can my brother Marcus not be with us in body anymore? This is not real life. This is some cruel nightmare.

The second stage of grief is anger. It can take many different forms. You may experience all forms or only one.

You may be angry with the person that has died, angry they left too soon, angry with yourself for not saying how you really felt, angry with the medical staff for not saving their life. You may be angry with God, something that many experience and begin to question your religious beliefs.

"The will to save a life is not the power to stop a death," Kubler-Ross explains. Anger is an indication of the love you have for the person that has died.

Feelings of anger can isolate you from family and friends when you need them the most. You may feel they are not there for you but in actual fact your feelings of suffering and loss tend to push them away. They have not abandoned you, they are allowing you to feel the anger and giving you time to process these feelings.

Anger toward yourself may also take the form of guilt. You may blame yourself and be angry that you didn't do something different that may have prevented the death.
"Anger affirms that you can feel, that you did love and that you have lost," says Kubler-Ross.

I experienced anger in different forms and at different times. I was struggling to understand my emotions. My anger towards Marcus was different to that with Dad. I was angry at the situation in which Marcus left. He was killed in a car accident. An accident that could have been prevented. I also became angry with my mother because she wouldn't stop crying and the sound of that caused me to storm from the house. It was so much to handle every single day.

Marcus' death also caused friction between my parents as they played the blame game. I became angry towards them and their fighting. Hadn't Marcus' death caused enough pain without adding more distress to our already tense and fraught situation?

I was so confused, hurt, angry, so broken. I felt all of these emotions almost immediately and simultaneously. But it was different because most of my life I'd visited Dad in hospitals. He was ill. And he suffered. In addition, to the death of my brother, it was all too much.

My parents were separated. My father did not live with my Mum and I. When he died, I found so many older wounds surfaced on my journey with grief. Some childhood issues came to pass. The anger at times was imploding. For this reason, I went and got professional help. I hated feeling so angry with Dad. It began to affect my everyday life. I sought professional counselling and began the process of resolving years of anger and other buried emotions and began to find peace. I was able to resolve years of anger and find peace.

The third stage in the grieving process is bargaining. This is when you plead with God or whomever it is you believe in. Questions such as, 'If you bring him back I will go to mass more, I will do more charity work' etc. Our everyday life becomes consumed in 'What if' and 'If only'.

We may even beg that we be taken and our loved one returned in our place. Parents who bury a child will usually plea for their life to be taken in place of the young child. It is also normal to ask for a sign that your loved one is in a safe and happy place or that you could hug them one last time.

We become stuck in the past. We want to do anything that will take away the pain and return our loved one. Bargaining can become an escape from the reality, pain and suffering, a distraction in life.

It almost pains me to relive what went through my head when it came to bargaining. I remember crying in my bed alone at night and asking God to take me instead, to bring Marcus back. Almost swap places. Everyone around me was so devastated that in my confused state I felt my family wouldn't be as sad if I were to be taken. Such a sorrowful thought at such a tender age.

But as time went on I realised that I had a purpose here and that I had my own life to live. I came to appreciate that my parents' grief would be very much the same if it was me who had passed.

Bargaining is a funny one because it is part of our everyday lives. Exam time, job interviews, the NCT centre, all places and moments in life we plead for what we want. But sometimes what we want isn't what is destined for us.

Following the stages of denial, anger and bargaining, you may fall into a state of sadness or as the fourth stage is referred to, depression. This is not a clinical depression that will be hanging over you for the remainder of your life. It is a reactive depression caused through grief.

It is extremely normal to feel this withdrawal from life and intense sadness. You may feel there is no reason to get out of bed, no energy or reason to leave the house.

Life feels pointless. Every task seems like an incredible effort that you would rather avoid. Social outings are no longer an option because you would be no fun, as you feel too sorry for yourself.

This feeling of sadness can come and go. An activity can help lift you from the slump and give a release of energy. When you are in a depressive state it is because your brain is low in serotonin, which is a chemical that releases the feelings of happiness. An hour of exercise a day releases serotonin in the brain and puts you in naturally a better mood according to studies in Harvard. "The benefits of exercise come directly from its ability to reduce insulin resistance, reduce inflammation, and stimulate the release of growth factors - chemicals in the brain that affect the health of brain cells, the growth of new blood vessels in the brain, and even the abundance and survival of new brain cells." (Harvard Medical School, 2016)

The depressive state can make you feel as though you are at rock bottom but with exercise and activities you will begin to see the light. When you are low and in a depressive state, the only way is up.

This stage was a very difficult time for me. I hit a wall head on and it really hurt. The feeling of sheer loneliness and darkness was almost indescribable. It is in itself a journey we must all face in our own time, and while may have support around us; it can be a lonely road.

In my case, I pushed everyone away even those who wanted to stay. I wanted to be left on my own. I didn't want to talk, didn't want to socialise, and didn't want to leave my bed. Even as I walked around busy streets I couldn't help but feel isolated. It got to a stage where I would walk back streets and quiet lanes just to avoid busier shop filled streets. I feared bumping into anyone I knew.

One day I was in the college medical centre to seek assistance for my troubled mental state. While in the waiting room a friend from home came in and immediately started chatting away. She asked me why I was in and I couldn't control it, I burst out crying and told her how sad I was feeling. A weight lifted and I felt her warmth.

I decided then that I needed to concentrate on me. I had to put myself first and I wanted to feel happiness again. From then, I studied grief, I read and learned more about this intricate world. It brought joy to my hardened soul to understand what was happening. I grew from it and it led me to the final stage.

The final stage of the grieving process is acceptance. For some this may take years to accept what has happened and begin to move forward. It usually takes something significant for this to occur.

Perhaps meeting a certain person, something you read that makes life clearer, and something that happens to you. The birth of a child or a new friendship could take you to this stage or an inquest that can close a case.

There is no time on acceptance and the individual must experience each stage of the grieving process to gain acceptance.

Once you can accept that your loved one is now in a happier place, you can move on and start living your life again. Don't ever be afraid to talk to someone professional, to reason, understand and let go. It took me years to understand what was happening and then more time to accept what had happened in my life. Travelling along the road of grief was liberating. It was in no way easy but it gave me a massive sense of who I am and what direction I wanted to go in. Even now, I am in control of who I am and know what I want. And that is happiness and zest for living.

The Road to Acceptance

For me, the road to acceptance took at least ten years following my brother's car crash. When it did begin to happen, I thought it couldn't be grief at this late stage. I found it hard to accept that grief could take so long to heal. In addition, I felt people would not believe me if I tried to explain the underlying reason for my depressive state. The day it hit me that my brother and father were dead was so unbearably painful. I cried and cried and could not stop. My heart was beyond broken. Thinking back on it all now, I can remember the physical pain that was going through that very heart.

Nothing could have prepared me for this. But my mother was by my side and she was ready for this moment. She knew what was happening. The loneliness that followed was extremely dark and I thought nothing or nobody will ever fill this hole but they did. The depression that fell over me was heavy and, at times, never ending, but I always had 'hope' within my reach. When Doctors prescribed medication I knew it wasn't the answer. I took them initially but deep down I knew I had to feel the pain and experience the darkness to fully appreciate the light and serenity. I began my journey and I was determined to sail through every ocean, rough and calm. Even as I type this I have elements of sadness but I now know that I can deal with this and continue on with a happy life.

Each stage of grief felt like a chapter in a book. I had to go through it page by page delicately and in my own time. The key message I wish to share with you, my reader, is that there is no time limit of grief, there is no right or wrong way. There is hope, there is support and there is life after death.

I'll share the story and poem of C.S. Lewis with you as a final parting. C.S. Lewis wrote the book, 'A Grief Observed', after the death of his wife, Joy Davidman in 1960. Writing became an outlet for Lewis to express his feelings of loss and suffering he endured at the death of his wife. The book is a reflection of his own experience of dealings with death. It is a compilation of four diaries that he composed while experiencing the different stages of grief. In the book he gives a detailed description of life without Joy and questions his beliefs in faith. It is an example of *double entendre*. When his wife, Joy, died, so did the joy he felt around him. In the below extract, Lewis speaks of the fear he feels. The feeling of loss for his wife has sent him into a dark and lonely place. He seems bewildered and confused of the world around him and struggles to understand where he belongs on this earth.

These feelings of loss and fear are reflected in the work of Kubler-Ross. And they are individual and unique to each person. Just as the sandy beach is made up of millions of grains of sand, so too is our grief comprised of a myriad of different emotions, some common, some unique. But the important message is that, even though we may all go through similar states of emotions, our own experience is totally unique and individual to us. The key message is that we need to be loved, held, respected and understood so that we can, like me, *survive* to enjoy each future day with hope and happiness.

"NO-ONE ever told me that grief felt so like fear.

I am not afraid but the sensation is like being afraid.

The same fluttering in the stomach, the same restlessness-

I keep on swallowing-

I find it hard to take in what anyone says, or perhaps hard to want to take it in-

Yet I want the others to be about me.

I dread the moments when the house is empty.

If only they would talk to one another and not to me."

C.S. Lewis - A Grief Observed

ALTERNATIVE HEALING

Over the years I have tried many different forms of healing. I've been to counsellors, psychologists, Doctors and I've even been put on anti-depressants. I have always been very open to trying new and different forms of therapy and often will revisit some areas because, while some days are better than others, I can feel the darkness come over me from time to time and instead of battling it alone I seek healing.

After spending almost a year on medication I always felt there was something deeper, more meaningful that could help me through my sad phase. Plus I hated that numbing feeling the tablets gave me. I always knew it was a short fix to a long-term problem. And I needed time to heal and grieve and also a more meaningful understanding as to what I was going through.

Since 2011 I have been to see so many special people, all who offer various forms of healing. I have always been very open and spiritual and anything or anyone that can offer even the slightest feeling of relief is worth it to me. When I was at my lowest I was desperate to be pulled from the pit of darkness. I couldn't always do it alone and needed help. I have never been afraid to go after it but haven't always known where to get it. My mother has sought most of the help for me. She has found some great people that have helped me over the years. While I appreciate not everything will work for everyone I do believe in trying out various forms of healing until you find the one that is right for you. Here are some of the people I have worked with over the years who have offered me healing, clarity and peace of mind.

Heidi Messenger, International Medium and Author

I heard about Heidi a couple of years ago, around 2012. A neighbour had been to see her and kept telling my mother that we should go visit her. We booked in and at the time it was five or six months until our appointment as she is extremely busy and popular. We almost forgot about it until we got a call to confirm. We were both nervous and a little apprehensive travelling to see her. She is a medium and the first I had ever visited.

Once we met her we knew she was special. She has this warmth and her eyes are welcoming and comforting. Mum and I had separate sessions. It is very hard to describe what happens during them. It is so powerful, emotional and special. Heidi told me things about my brother and father that nobody could have known. They relayed messages to her for me and I honestly felt like for the first time in years I could hear them speak back to me.

At the time I was unemployed and really lost. That period after leaving college can be very daunting. Some friends secured jobs before they even finished lectures, so I put this unnecessary pressure on myself. I felt useless because I was back living at home and doing nothing with my life. Heidi said she could see me in a city office, a large building with a glass façade. I had no idea what she meant as I was living in Ardrahan and had no intentions of going anywhere.

I left that day feeling very drained but something changed within me. For the first time in a long time I felt it was okay to smile again and it gave me a zest to get on and live my life. In fact Marcus made a comment about my life, he said I had become boring to watch. Perhaps I had become too scared and sad to go out and do anything for myself. After that, I made sure to start living my own life and that I did.

In March 2013 I got an email from MTV inviting me to London for an interview for an internship with the news team. Two weeks later I moved to London and began working in a large building with a glass façade in Camden Town. I travelled, moved country, started to build a career and everything I did I felt made them proud and my life less boring. I love a challenge and the fact that Marcus said that about me made me eager to prove him wrong.

Now I know some people don't believe in healers and medium-ship and each to their own but the relief that Heidi brought to mum and I was amazing. She had a massive role to play in our healing. She brought us peace and reassurance and I think if anyone can relieve the pain of grief then I welcome them with open arms. I went to see Heidi again when I moved back to Ireland and she just made everything clearer. I am guilty of having no patience and always expecting things to happen now. And when my plans and ideas didn't come into fruition straight away I would get down and upset and feel like a failure. Good things come to those who wait was something I had to train my mind to believe. Heidi helped with this and was able to give me patience.

Heidi is a medium, healer and intuitive advisor. Basically though like a radio - translating messages, and a chance to confirm that there is still a relationship after passing, validating that a person's loved ones are watching over them with love and protection. The healing comes from being a 'safe' place to open up and share their feelings and encourage them to believe in themselves and in their potential. It is not intended to take the place of a therapist and sometimes it is suggested they seek further help should they need it. It is quite hard to put in a sentence as every reading, as every person (and indeed their spirit families) is unique.
You can find Heidi on Facebook – Heidi Messenger

Teresa Spelman

I was first introduced to Teresa during the Christmas of 2013. I was home from London and I was very down in myself. My mother read about her in the local newspaper and rang her up. Within no time she called to our house and she did some healing with me. It was so lovely to be able to do this in my own home. The living room is filled with photos of Marcus and she lit candles. My cat Baba refused to leave the room and she took that as a sign when she heard his name. Sai Baba of Shirdi was an Indian spiritual healer and Teresa has spent much time in India.

She was the first person to teach me yoga and said it would be so beneficial. I always thought it was just a good form of stretching. We started with some basic moves and she had me practicing every morning and night, just three stretches. It was very doable and I got into a great routine while living in London. I found it really great and started to feel better going to work and it helped with relaxing at night. She also helped me with my diet and we brought it back to basic vegetables and grains. It was the first time I started to really take care of my body and mind.

She also taught me how to meditate. Before this I could never be alone in my mind. I had to always be busy and there had to be noise. I couldn't zone out for fear of what I would really hear and feel. I knew at times that my mind was a volcano ready to erupt and for years I was trying to avoid it, hoping it was dormant. But it wasn't. And from 2011, it was starting to spit volcanic ash. I knew this was going to be massive when it did eventually burst.

In London I was in a very dark place. I loved work because it was a distraction and I was too busy to think while in the Hawley Crescent studios. Camden Town is chaotic and that too helped to keep my mind distracted. Teresa came to visit me in London to show me that I could meditate and be in silence no matter where in the world I was.

She taught me various meditation chants and I began trying them out. Sometimes it would result in my crying but this was clearing the blockages. I kept what I was doing very private at the time because people around me didn't understand. A guy from the office made a sarcastic comment about people who meditate and I wasn't going to let anyone take me down, especially when I was already there.

I really enjoyed that time of yoga and meditation and it being part of my every day. When I moved to Dublin in August of 2014 the yoga slipped away, but I have started to do it again. I have kept up meditation but I know I can and will do more because now I am stronger and ready to explore it more and deeper. It is truly powerful.

Teresa feeds people what they need, be it listening with an open heart and no judgement, yoga, emotional support, food, a cup of tea, a retreat in nature or a fresh perspective on life. Teresa trained in India as a yoga teacher and naturopathy Doctor. She offers people the opportunity to relax and rejuvenate at the Willow Retreat in the West of Ireland.

You can find more information at www.thewillowretreat.com or search The Willow Retreat on Facebook and Instagram.

Elaine Molloy – Indigo Light Medical Healer

I've known Elaine for some time now and we have always had a connection. I am drawn to her kind nature and warm heart and I didn't realise that there was a reason behind all of this – Elaine is a healer and the person who would help me in more ways than I ever expected.

When I first went for healing with Elaine I was very lost and confused. I had moved home from London and wasn't sure of the job I was in or what direction I wanted my life to take. Not long into that session she could see my broken heart and the affect that my brother's and father's death had on me. All factors to my confusion at that time.

I went on to do more sessions with Elaine and each time I felt a weight lift, a sigh of relief and a sense of calmness around me. It was so great to have someone who really understood my loss, and at that time, my anguish.

Over the past few months I have felt a shift take place in my mind. It is as though the grief has been lifted and I can now enjoy my life. My anxiety is under control and now the things that were once a burden or a task are now an enjoyment – I even have a better understanding of what it is I want to do with my life.

Recently, Elaine and I did a distance healing reading, meaning I sent her some questions and she did the work from her home while I stayed in mine and the answers to my queries blew me away. The doubts I had are now diminished. I feel confident about my current situation and the direction my life is going to take.

Elaine explained every aspect of the reading to me, what happened during it and details about my life. At the time that she was doing the reading I could feel the energy. I felt quite lethargic and lay down for a little while and after the session I felt the energies change.

Even certain things Elaine said to me from previous sessions are starting to formulate in real life. It is amazing to now see what she could see for me.

Elaine is an intuitive healing guide with 20 years of experience in helping people to heal using natural methods and remedies along with profound energy healing treatments. Elaine works as a medium to spirit in all aspects of health and healing channeling through her exactly what the client needs to know or hear for their highest healing. This information may include anything from dietary advice, herbs, supplements and lifestyle changes to communication with deceased loved ones in order to bring about healing and release at the deepest level.

You can find more at www.elainemolloy.com or on Facebook Indigo Light Medical Intuitive Healer

Pieta House/ Counselling Services

As mentioned I went to Pieta House in October 2015. At the time I had slipped into a very dark place and it was my mother who drove me to the centre in Tuam. I remember that drive so well because I knew where I was going. The house was lovely and warm and very inviting. I felt like I was in someone's living room, I felt safe. I was seen by a nurse and assessed and it was decided that I would begin a programme almost immediately.

I went twice a week for a few weeks and then it went to once a week. I had the most wonderful counsellor. He was superb. I looked forward going every week. I drove myself to Tuam for each session after my initial assessment. I would arrive early to have coffee and biscuits, which are always provided. I met some really wonderful people in that room, all there for the same reason. There was this understanding between us all.

When it came to the final session I cried so much because I was sad I wouldn't be returning, not because I felt down. I had come on leaps and bounds in those sessions and now my time had come to put everything into practice.

I've never been shy of talking to professionals. I spoke to someone while in NUIG and I even spoke to someone more recently in Limerick. If I feel myself slipping again I will go back to counselling because money spent on those sessions is an investment into my mental health and wellbeing.

Alternative Medicine

When I moved back home to Galway in 2015, my mother was trying out some alternative healing and Chinese medicine. I gave it a go as well because I am willing to try anything that will help any blockage mentally and physically.

I have tried Reiki, Acupuncture, Massages and Reflexology. All have been interesting and helpful. I really enjoy learning about the connection between body and mind and if anything, it is a nice relaxing break.

Incense and oils have been of great benefit to me as well. I always have Rescue Remedy close at hand and lavender beside my bed. Most nights I shake some lavender drops on my pillow and sheets and I find the scent to be relaxing and aiding in a good night's sleep. I light incense during the day and evening. Nag Champa is one of my favourites. It really sets the mood for meditating as well. I have a Himalayan salt lamp in my bedroom that I use also. Its dimly lit orange light is warming and apparently they improve air quality. I recently got some plants and I love how they make the place look, and keeping them alive is a small and rewarding challenge.

MARCUS SCULLY

Marcus grew, pillared by love,
From all he knew.

There is no measure of a breath,
Its deep intake fuelling the external senses,
Preparing for vision; beyond.

There is no measure of a soaring heartbeat,
Its soft sound fuelling a rugby ball
High off the ground.

There is no measure for eighteen years,
As smiles of joy sparkle in young fresh eyes
And cheers of love loudly call his name

On playing pitches far and near.
The referee felt fleeting time and swiftly
His whistle blew.

There is no measure of a last breath,
Fuelling the internal senses
Preparing for vision; beyond.

Only breath changes
As it goes out of itself,
Towards the ultimate goal.

Marcus grew to be a pillar of love,
To all he knew.

By a close family friend, Máire.

THIS IS ME

In March 2011, I shared my first ever public post about what I was feeling and experiencing. At the time, I was studying a Master's in Journalism in NUI Galway. For years, I kept my feelings tucked away in my weary heart and shared them only with a pen and paper, just for my eyes. Not even my closest friends knew what I was hiding. I suffered what I call a break through during that year in Galway and sharing that blog was the most difficult, yet ground-breaking, thing I did for myself and for others. It is subsequently the reason I bring you this book. When people began reading what I had shared, I realised I was not alone, so many of us suffer in silence. Every day. I hope my story can help you on your own journey.

*****

I lay on the cold dark floor, lost, confused, bruised and broken. Had the end come? At the age of 22, was this what I had become? I was lonely, but not alone. The pain in my chest held me on that floor. I was zapped from my comatose state by the sound of fluttering and as I raised my head I saw white feathers surrounding my weak body. I followed the fluttering sound to the window. And there he was. A beautiful butterfly eagerly wanting to be set free. I struggled to get the window open and allow him begin his journey of freedom. I watched as he opened his great black and orange wings and set on his maiden voyage.

For the first time in weeks it became clear. I set the butterfly free so now it was time to set myself free. I have spent 7 years now holding on to a life I used to live. A life that seemed perfect for me. One in which I was surrounded by my mother, father and brother.

Life dealt me a great blow and God took the people I loved the most away from me. My mother was heartbroken and suddenly I had to bottle my tears because I felt I could not let her see a sad and lonely girl. She needed me and she needed me to be strong, or so I thought.

As the years went by I became this strong woman. I was the leader of the pack, the life and soul of every party and I was loving life. In September 2011, I began my Master's in NUIG. Another new chapter, new people and new opportunities. Surely this was my year of dreams and a great new step in my new life. As the weeks went by I began to get sick. I couldn't keep food down. I became erratic. My social life kick started and going out three or four times a week was my new lifestyle. Each party was as great as the next. Preparing for the nights out was just as important as the night itself.

The day after the night before was when I first began to notice a change in myself. Staying in bed all day was my preferred option. Did I have the perfect life? I thought so. Coming up to Christmas I took another change in my life. I pushed the people I loved the most away because I had a new exciting life and those who didn't want to join me on the dance floor I didn't need. I went out and made new friends and ditched my old ones. I was in self-destruct mode and I wasn't thinking of the consequences or of the feelings of those around me. If someone I had just met through a college lecture or event asked me to go on a night out, I went without any hesitation.

The Christmas was spent with a glass in my hand as the partying continued night after night. Everyone said to stay in, but what was the fun in that? Who would I meet sitting on the couch? I needed someone in my life that I could care for so I could ignore my own pain. Instead, I came out of my skin pleading to find someone to fill that loneliness and in turn pushed people away. The following day I was left feeling alone, upset and torn.

I let this cycle continue for weeks into 2012 until one day I woke up and realised I had to look after myself. I couldn't stop crying and there was a pain in my heart as I sobbed. My mother and aunt had to come into me in Galway. Each tear was only an expression of my loss. Was this the end of me?

No, it was the beginning of the rest of my life. For, that day as I lay on the floor, I realised that Marcus and Dad were dead. I had to accept that for the first time in my life. I was not suffering from any disease. Medication wasn't the answer. I had to cleanse my soul of the pain I had ignored for so long. That meant crying. And, boy, did I cry.

Grief comes in five stages. Denial is the first. I have been in denial for years about the loss I suffered. Anger was a stage that I went through also. I was so angry with God for taking them from me, angry with my mother for crying so much, angry with myself. I tried bargaining. That is the third stage. I begged for some sign that Marcus and Dad were happy. I begged for my own happiness. A quick fix some might say. The fourth stage is depression, which is something I had never before experienced in my life. I was so frightened to admit what I was feeling. I bottled it up but eventually the bottle was so full it couldn't take anymore and wanted to overflow. I fought to prevent it from bursting open. It resulted in me puking, having severe stomach problems and prevented me from sleeping and concentrating on college work.

I started to attend counselling. Even in counselling I gave out about everyone that wasn't there for me, that wouldn't be nice to me, who didn't hear my call. But they did hear my call. In fact they saw and heard it before me.

The road to acceptance is the fifth stage of grieving. It is possibly the hardest stage to comprehend. I have spent seven years living a life that I thought was fulfilling. I wasn't just living my own life, I was living a life for Marcus and Dad. But they have gone to their place of rest. They have lived their lives and their time on earth was over. I had to stop living their life, I had to live my own.

Releasing that butterfly into the open world allowed me to accept who I am. I had to set Marcus and Dad free and so now I had to pick myself up off the cold dark ground, spread my wings and follow the light of life.